The Pocket Scroll Series

SHAAR PRESS

Parenting

published by

SHAAR PRESS

by Design

The 5-Level Method for Raising Younger Children

Rabbi
Yisrael Kleinman
LMSW

שמואל קמנצקי

Rabbi S. Kamenetsky

2018 Upland Way
Philadelphia, PA19131

Home: 215-473-2798
Study: 215-473-1212

בס״ד, אסרו חג השבועות תשע״ה

לכבוד ידידי הרב המופלג ר׳ ישראל יוסף בן ידידי הרה״ג ר׳
אברהם צבי הכהן קליינמאן שליט״א,

קבלתי ספרו העוסק בעניני חינוך, שמטרתו להורות דרך
ומסילה בחינוך הבנים, ומידי עברי בו ראיתי שכב׳ סלל דרך ישר
בדרכי חינוך הבנים, וניכר בדבריו הרבה עמל ויגיעה ומחשבה עמוקה.

והנה כבר איתמחי גברא בסיועו להרבה אנשים בעצה ותושי׳,
שידוע לי הצלחתו הגדולה בס״ד בתחום זה, וכעת מפיץ מעיינותיו
לסייע להורים המבקשים דרך ישר בחינוך ילדיהם, ודבר טוב הוא
להפיצו לרבים שיהנו ממנו ויהיה לתועלת.

במיוחד נהניתי מאד ממה שכב׳ האריך בגנות הכעס, שמפורסם
וידוע לכל העוסקים בחינוך שהכעס הוא מהמזיקים הגדולים לנפשות
הילדים, וכיון שבא המחנך לכלל כעס בודאי לא ישיג מבוקשתו כלל,
ומאד מאד צריכים ליזהר להתרחק ממדה מגונה הלזו, ויפה האריך
להראות גנות הכעס ולשלול אותו מדרכי החינוך.

יזכה כב׳ להמנות ממזכי הרבים שצדקתם עומדת לעד, וברכתי
להרבה הצלחה ונחת מכל המשפחה.

Table of Contents

Part IV: The Liebowitz Family

Acknowledgments

Despite the fact that I'm the recorded author of this book, it was truly a group effort.

First, I would like to thank my dear father, Rabbi Heshy Kleinman *shlit"a*, who is by far the most prolific author in a family of writers. Abba, you encouraged me to write this book; you helped me every step of the way, and without that help and encouragement this book would never have come to light. Mommy, you have stood by Abba's side as he has written his *sefarim*, and have always been there for me at the most crucial of moments. Thank you.

My dear father- and mother-in-law, Dr. Jay and Dr. Mindy Rosenblum, you have always treated me as one of your children, not merely as an in-law, and have been there to help in any way you could at all times. Thank you.

Another crucial person in the creation of this book is my editor, Mrs. Chana Nestlebaum. You took the raw material and ideas I gave you and through your incredible mastery of the art of wordsmithing have woven them into a compelling and readable book. Without you I would still be stuck on Chapter 2. May Hashem grant you many more years of productive and masterful writing.

Thank you to the expert professional team at ArtScroll, who took a raw manuscript and transformed it into a full-fledged book: Mrs. Judi Dick, for her masterful editing as well as her insightful comments on the content; Mrs. Estie Dicker for corrections to the manuscript; Eli Kroen for his beautiful cover design; Mrs. Rivky Kapenstein for the eye-pleasing layout; and Mrs. Faygie Weinbaum for her meticulous proofreading. Thank you as well to Mendy Herzberg for coordinating the project, and to Rabbi Avrohom Biderman for taking the book from beginning to end with tremendous enthusiasm and support.

To my dear friends and "idea *chavrusos*" with whom I have had privilege of consulting and working through the concepts that are presented in this book: Through your penetrating analysis and precise questions, I was compelled to sharpen my thinking and tighten my ideas. Rabbi Shlomo Yehuda Wajsbort, and Rabbi Amram Ben Attar. Thank you.

Even the best ideas must be field-tested to verify that they work not only in theory but in reality as well. And so, thank you to all of my clients over the past several years, those of you who have trusted me by sharing your inner world, and who have been kind enough to let me know when things *weren't* working. Thank you as well to the members of the

Sunday-night parenting Vaad in Kollel Ner Avrohom. You came faithfully week after week, and challenged me to make sure that my ideas were presented in a way that was clear and understandable.

A special thank-you to Maran Harav Shmuel Kamenetsky *shlit"a*, who has always been available to answer all my difficult personal and professional *shailos* over the years. His warmth, wisdom and kindness have helped me though many a difficult decision. May he be *zocheh* to be *manhig* Klal Yisrael with *gezunt ad bi'as goel tzedek*. Thank you as well to Harav Sholom Kamenetsky *shlit"a*, who has made himself available day or night to help with *chizuk* and *hadrachah* in the difficult halachic *shailos* that often arise in the field of mental health.

Thank you to my sweet *kinderlach* Serach, Shmuel, Chaim, Dovid and Rena for lighting up my life. May you all be *zocheh* to *shtieg* in Torah, *avodah* and *gemilas chasadim* and grow up to be a *nachas* to us and to Hashem.

A special thank-you to my dear wife and partner Rochel, for always being there with grace and kindness to do everything necessary for me to have the time and space to work on my multiple projects, and for being willing to pick up the slack with graciousness and good humor. May we be *zocheh* to many more years of *avodas Hashem, gezunt* and *nachas*, together.

Leaving best for last, thank you Hashem for everything. As we say in *Nishmas, "ilu finu malei shirah kayam."* There are not enough words to express my thanks for the amount of *chessed*, *berachah* and goodness with which You have showered me with throughout the years and in every waking moment. All I can say is *Hatov ki lo chalu rachamecha, v'hamirachem ki lo samu chasadecha.*

Yisrael Kleinman

Iyar 5776
May 2016

Prologue

If you are reading this book, your choice is evidence that you possess the most essential piece of wisdom necessary for a parent; success requires effort. We are not born with an innate understanding of how to how to raise a family.

If we are inordinately blessed, we grow up in a well-run family and learn from our own parents the skills we will need. We grow up with a healthy sense of responsibility, personal boundaries, self-discipline and trust in ourselves, and we are able to apply all these tools to raising our own children along the same path. Most people, however, need to learn at least some of these skills on the job.

Everyone knows that raising a family is hard work. What people do not consider, however, is that not all hard work is equal. Some aspects of work bring joy and satisfaction, while others breed sadness and frustration. For instance, if you are a storeowner, you are happy to do the work of finding good inventory sources and planning marketing strategies. You would feel far less satisfaction dealing with irate creditors or unhappy customers. Both tasks are hard work, but the former tasks are energizing. The latter tasks are the draining consequences of an inefficiently run business. If they were the only activities you did every day, with no time left for the more satisfying tasks, you would neither enjoy nor succeed in running the store.

In raising our families, there are many instances where we feel the joy and satisfaction we crave. Nonetheless getting children through the routines of the day, dealing with fighting, messiness, poor sleeping and eating practices, homework and so forth can take so much of our energy that we have nothing left for the real goals of building healthy, happy, functional human beings. These challenges can rob our faces of the smiles our children need to see and rob our bodies of the energy we need to be proactive, engaged parents. They can even spark anger and resentment that poison the atmosphere of our homes.

The method outlined in this book has been used successfully by numerous families to reverse this debilitating trend. The goal is not to make parenting less work; it is to help parents pour their effort into a constructive, satisfying endeavor. It is to help them stop spinning their wheels and finally head in the right direction. You will expend as much or more energy with this method, but you won't feel depleted. On the contrary, you will feel fulfilled and energized.

To be sure, this is not the book to end all parenting challenges. Life is too fluid for one-stop solutions. New babies, new stages in life, health problems, issues at school or with friends and so much more can arise to change the dynamics and require parents to once again face challenges they thought they had already addressed successfully. However, with the consistent use of the Five-Level Parenting method, you'll be able to click right into action, equipped with the tools to handle the new challenge.

Before beginning to learn Five-Level Parenting, here is a glimpse of what you can realistically expect to achieve:

You've been working for months on establishing a stable, organized household. Your children are becoming cooperative and responsible. They know what is expected of them and they feel your consistent, firm and loving involvement in their lives. They are getting along better with one another and the atmosphere of your home is greatly improved.

You know things are better, but you don't realize how much better until you visit your parents for Shabbos. Your brother's family is also visiting, and his children are behaving much as yours previously did. You note how the parents issue orders to the children but don't follow through. You see how they give in to the children time and again, only to end up screaming at them in frustration.

When the children are asked to help clear the table after the meal, your nieces and nephews slip away as if no one had said a word. Your sister-in-law calls them back, but she doesn't really expect them to come. She yells after them that they should be ashamed of themselves for not helping Bubbi.

Meanwhile, you've assigned each of your children a specific task to help clear the table. They get busy right away. One child balks, so you start counting to three; he knows there'll be a time-out awaiting him if he doesn't get moving. He runs back to the table and joins in the effort. You lavish the children with praise for their helpfulness and offer to take them to the park as a reward. "Hashem must love you," your brother remarks. "He gave you little angels."

You don't say what you're thinking: *These aren't angels. We've been working on this for months.*

Five-level Parenting is effective. Nonetheless as time goes on, you'll have a day when your energy flags and you let things get out of hand. As soon as you feel that old sense of frustration building in you, you'll summon your energy and grab hold of your parenting tools. You'll have setbacks; your children will have setbacks. But you will see that your family is moving forward. You and your spouse will feel confident in setting goals because you have the means to reach them. Best of all, your children will feel down to their core that they deserve your very best efforts.

I want every reader to know that I have seen these changes with my own eyes. Many times, with many types of parents. The soft-spoken and the aggressive, the organized and the disorganized, the logical and the emotional, the energetic and the laid-back — everyone can use these techniques and succeed. It is my hope that in sharing this information with a wider audience, many more parents will feel the joy and satisfaction that family life can and should bring, and many more children will reap the benefits.

Part I:
Another Parenting Book?

Introduction

S*himmy," Malki called to her 6-year-old son. "Come on, get up! I gave you five extra minutes already. Let's not miss the bus!"*

The blanket shifted abruptly. Various lumps and bumps beneath it rose and fell. A groan emerged from somewhere within the heap.

"Oh, no, Hashem, no!" Malki whispered to herself. "Shimmy's for sure going to miss the bus again this morning. What am I going to do?"

"Come on, Shimmy," she said firmly. "Remember we said last night that you were going to get up nicely today? Mommy will be so proud of you if you get on the bus with the other kids like a big boy."

Behind Malki's sweet voice was a frantic, internal voice. "I absolutely cannot be late to work again today. My boss is going to go nuts. I'm going to get fired! I can't have a 6-year-old running the show!"

"My stomach hurts," Shimmy croaked dramatically.

"Oh, that must be uncomfortable," Malki forced herself to say. "As soon as you're dressed, I'll give you some hot cocoa and I'll bet it will feel better. Let's go. Here's your shirt and pants."

He lay still as a stone. Malki began dressing him but he stiffened and made the process as difficult as possible. She knew he was having trouble adjusting to the stricter routines of first grade. He was a sweet boy who just liked to play and color and have fun; sitting still and learning was coming hard.

But it was time to get on with the program! The family needed Malki's income and she could not come in late every morning because Shimmy had to be driven to school. And what about kibbud av v'eim? This resistance could turn into a habit that would bring no end of trouble as he got older. The whole situation had to end right now!

Malki felt her temper rising.

"Shimmy!" she yelled. "I'm your mother and you have to listen to me! I'm not having a lazy, spoiled little boy in this house! You get up now or you're going to bed tonight right after supper and there'll be no playtime for you! You're driving Mommy crazy. Is that what you want? You better be downstairs dressed in five minutes!" She walked out, shutting the door firmly behind her.

The blast of anger brought tears to Shimmy's eyes. He solemnly got dressed and went to the kitchen to eat the breakfast Malki had prepared. As she watched him nibble sadly at his cereal, she was overwhelmed with remorse. The poor little boy — what did he know about irate bosses and household budgets?

She put a hand on his shoulder. "Shimmy, thank you for listening. I'm sorry about yelling at you. I love you and you're a good boy."

Shimmy still looked wilted as he left for the bus stop. "There's got to be a better way to do this," Malki thought.

This is a book for Malki, and for every parent who finds that real-time parenting does not always go by the books. No matter what a person's parenting philosophy is — authoritarian or friendly, demanding or accepting, rigid or flexible or anything in between — the interactions of daily life can easily push our theories aside and leave us standing there, like Malki, being buffeted by a situation that is out of our control.

That is the problem, because when a person feels he has lost control, his reaction is to panic. At that point, everything deteriorates. Tempers rise and then shouting, screaming, harsh words and physical force rush onto the scene before anyone has a chance to think. The harm that can be done in these heated few moments is inestimable. The harsh words hurt. The parent-child relationship frays, sometimes to the breaking point. As a therapist, I have seen the long-term fallout from panic parenting in full-grown adults who are still nursing the grievances of their childhoods.

However, not all parenting challenges come from the type of situation we just illustrated. Some come from the opposite direction: a parent takes a hands-off approach to some issue that really does require attention. For instance, if in the above scenario, what if day after day, Malki allowed Shimmy to stay home? What if she reasoned that, if he really didn't want to go, she would just wait until he got bored enough to return on his own? Since Malki and Shimmy are fictional, we really cannot state what the outcome of that strategy would be. Theoretically, however, most parents would agree that Shimmy would lose a great deal, both in terms of schooling and in terms of self-discipline and growth. Therefore his parents need to find some method whereby to ensure his attendance.

But what is it they should do? The purpose of this book is to help parents answer these real-time questions confidently, in the moment. As you will learn, the key to parenting is to know what you are trying to accomplish. Once you have identified your goal, you can access the right tools for the job. You're equipped — ready, willing and able — to handle whatever comes along. You might still have a struggle on your hands, but you never need to panic. You never need to fight, nor do you ever need to throw up your hands in defeat.

Five-Level parenting is a system that identifies five overall parenting goals. All our interactions with our children are aimed at one or more of these goals. Each of these goals calls for its own approach. For instance, Malki's scream might have been the right approach if she were trying to stop Shimmy from injuring his sister. However, if the goal is to instill in him a sense of responsibility or obedience, that tool was ineffective.

The chapters ahead will show you how to analyze the challenges you face with your own children and classify them within the five-level structure. Then, this five-level plan will guide you to access tools you can use, tools that fit into your family's own lifestyle and philosophy, to strive toward the goals you have for your children.

In the wide world of parenting programs, this one is among the simplest. We all know that we cannot use a hammer to turn a screw or a fork to eat our soup; there is no great innovation in stating that we need to know what we want to accomplish before we can pick the right tool for the job. This method has worked for the many, many parents who have attended to my parenting groups, used my workbook or consulted me on an individual basis. In just a few sessions, they experience a sense of relief and joy. Knowing where we are going and how to get there allows us to enjoy the journey.

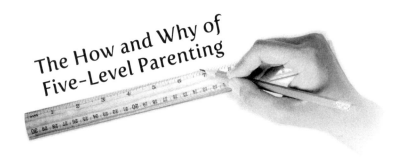

The How and Why of Five-Level Parenting

As parents, we live moment to moment. We are constantly being called upon to improvise a response to the situation in front of us. While we certainly have our routines and some idea of how our children will behave in various situations, the prevailing rule in parenting is "expect the unexpected." Because so many of our day-to-day parenting challenges are unexpected, we respond out of instinct, drawing upon:

- the parenting style we absorbed from our parents
- our own set of attitudes and beliefs
- the attitudes and beliefs of our community
- our present mood and basic nature.

In the opening scenario of stressed-out Malki and her uncooperative little boy, we saw what can happen when we are not prepared to meet a challenging situation. Malki needed to be on time for work and her son was doing everything he could to miss the bus and force her to drive him to school. She did not know what to do, but she had to do something. Reacting out of raw emotion, her words threatened and insulted her son, basically bullying him into cooperation.

In my practice, most parenting difficulties I encounter come from this sense of panic. Even parents who have done their homework by attending parenting classes or reading parenting books often find that when life happens, they are still thrashing around for a useful response. They may try to use the responses they've learned, but often enough, it doesn't work. Then they are truly at a loss and more desperate than ever.

In fact, Malki in our scenario started off with some good parenting techniques. She had apparently discussed the situation with her son the previous night, when things were calm. She gave him the positive reinforcement of being seen as a big boy if he got on the bus on time. She validated his complaint of a stomachache and showed sympathy. Then, when he still wouldn't budge and she was out of techniques, she blew her top.

There is a solution to this problem, and I have seen it work for nearly every family I have had the privilege of helping. That solution is to accurately pinpoint which of five overall parenting goals we are trying to achieve in our interaction with our child.

The five levels are:

- Level 1: avoiding significant irrevocable damage;
- Level 2: avoiding "normal" damage at the moment;
- Level 3: eliminating improper behaviors and developing proper skills and habits;

- Level 4: instilling important values in the child;
- Level 5: helping the child learn to process emotions, feel loved and be emotionally healthy.

Once a parent has identified which of these goals he seeks to accomplish in a given situation, he can access the right tools for the job. For example, a mother might wish to get her daughter to make her bed every morning. She discusses the benefits of orderliness with her daughter and listens attentively to her daughter's point of view, validating her feeling that she is rushed in the morning and no one sees her room anyway. Nevertheless, the mother insists that this is important and the daughter agrees to try. The next day, the bed remains unmade. Another discussion ensues that evening. The next day, the daughter makes her bed, but by the following day, she's already abandoned the task.

The mother's empathy and calm, firm rule-setting does not work. However, it is not because the technique is flawed, but rather, because it is being used to accomplish a goal it is not fit to accomplish. The mother might now say, "Ah! I've tried this focused listening and reflecting and empathizing stuff and it got me nowhere!" She may feel at a loss, and so she reverts to anger and scolding, which appear to work, at least for the short term. The question she needs to ask herself before the interaction even begins is, *What am I trying to accomplish and can active listening achieve that goal?*

To understand how this method applies, let's first define the five levels more completely. We can then use Malki's scenario to illustrate what types of challenges fit within each level.

Level 1: Emergency Response

Protecting a child's life is a parent's most immediate and non-negotiable concern. A child who endangers himself or others must be stopped in the fastest, most effective way possible. Furthermore, the child must receive a strong, unequivocal message that this behavior may never be repeated. What are some situations that fall within this level?

- An older child is about to hurt an infant.
- A small child is about to walk out into the street.
- A toddler has climbed on a chair and is trying to turn on the flame.
- A child is playing with a box of matches.
- A child refuses to put on a seatbelt in the car or a helmet while biking.

What these situations have in common is the irrevocable damage that could result from the child's behavior. We can't undo the tragic injuries or, *chas v'shalom*, death, that could result, and therefore, the very second the dangerous behavior comes to our attention, we must make it stop. In this case, the "nuclear option" is the right tool, because we must frighten the child away from ever attempting the behavior again, even when we are not watching.

Now let's look at Malki's situation. Is there a Level 1 goal she needs to accomplish? While her son's reluctance to go to school and the impact it is having on Malki's job could have serious long-term repercussions, no one would say that serious injury or death might result from him missing the bus that day.

The reaction she displayed — the harsh scolding — was a misuse of the nuclear option. Not only did it not address her real goals, but it may have diluted the power of a harsh response when it really might become appropriate in some other situation. If Mommy screams whenever things don't go her way, her screaming ceases to mean "Danger! Stop!"

Level 2: Immediate Imperatives

Not all immediate challenges are life threatening. Many are simply in-the-moment situations that must change for the good of the child, the parents or the people around them. Stubborn toddlers are especially adept at presenting Level 2 challenges, but older children can present them as well. Some situations we would classify within this level include:

- A child throws a tantrum in a public place.
- A child refuses to do some necessary routine activity such as getting up and dressed in the morning, going to bed on time, cleaning up something he spilled, doing homework.
- A child refuses to go with the parent on a necessary trip, outing or errand.
- A child throws a tantrum at the doctor's or dentist's office.
- A child behaves in a noisy, rowdy way at home or in a public place.

These situations all call for some immediate response. Our households and communities need order and routine to function, and we can't allow our children to turn it all upside down. Not only do these behaviors disturb people and keep them from doing what they need to do, but they also develop a self-centered, unregulated mentality in the child, who then grows up with an implicit worldview of "I can do whatever I please."

Nevertheless, they are not life-and-death emergencies. If we respond to these fairly regular challenges the way we respond to a Level 1 emergency, we defeat ourselves in three ways. First of all, the challenging behavior might only escalate, causing us to have to scream louder and threaten more dire consequences while the child digs his heels in deeper. Secondly, to pull out the "nuclear option" for daily challenges makes our daily interactions far too explosive for love and security to thrive. Thirdly, as we noted above, overusing a Level 1 response disables it.

Looking back at Malki's and Shimmy's unhappy morning ritual, we see that the primary challenge falls neatly into the Level 2 category. Malki clearly feels that a situation must change right away, within minutes, before Shimmy is too late to catch his bus. The immediacy of a Level 2 challenge is clear, and so is the routine, normal nature of the challenge.

Malki plunges into "emergency mode" not because there is a real life-and-death emergency, but because she is extrapolating from a normal parent-child issue a whole litany of terrible repercussions. In her view, she is not just facing a first-grader who doesn't want to get up. She's facing being fired from her job, followed by financial ruin. She is not just dealing with her child's momentary stubbornness; she is dealing with a transgression of the Fifth Commandment, leading straight into rebelliousness and untold misery.

She may agree that there is no need, nor any benefit, in harshly scolding her son over his difficulty adjusting to first grade. However, the other issues do seem to justify her response. Should she let him get away with disobeying her? With disobeying the Torah? Can she let him put her job at risk? When she sees the situation as desperate and life-altering, adrenalin takes over and an explosion is almost inevitable.

If Malki could have analyzed the situation in terms of her real goals as she stood there in her son's bedroom at 7:30 on a Tuesday morning, she would have seen that the only issue she could effectively address at the moment was the immediate one of getting Shimmy out the door on time. She would have already prepared a tool for accomplishing that goal, and she would have used it calmly and effectively. Shimmy would have eaten his breakfast without tears in his eyes, and Malki would have spared herself a heart full of guilt.

Level 3: Breaking and Building Habits

Much of parenting is about training. We want our children to overcome the destructive, negative habits that often come naturally to them (and us) and develop in their place the positive, constructive habits that build a productive life. Often, by building positive habits, we can eliminate many of the Level 2 challenges that arise. Daily routines can be completed without friction. On a more advanced level, we can instill positive social habits as well, teaching children to express gratitude and be helpful.

Level 3 goals include teaching children to refrain from:

- Carelessness
- Speaking in a loud voice
- Interrupting others
- Using others' belongings without permission

- Whining and kvetching
- Fighting
- Forgetting homework or other items
- Procrastinating

On the positive side, parents can instill many positive habits in their children, which will not only make them more pleasant and successful children, but will serve them well for life. Some of the positive habits parents teach their children include:

- Caring for themselves
- Keeping to a schedule
- Completing tasks
- Organization
- Appropriate, polite behavior
- Appreciating and handling money
- Caring for belongings
- Respecting others' belongings and space

The common thread in all of these habits, both the positive and the negative, is that they cannot be acquired quickly. If we see that a child needs to develop or shed a certain habit, we have to dig in for the long run. Time and consistency are our most powerful tools.

There are specific techniques for training children into and out of habits, which we will explore later, but the overall mind-set for Level 3 parenting is that of training. It is a long-term process that includes a plan, goal-setting and reinforcement over the course of time. It's a curriculum, not a one-shot lecture.

Looking again at Malki's situation, we can see that there were a few potential Level 3 goals that might help Shimmy develop the strengths he needs to succeed in first grade. There might possibly be some unhelpful bedtime habits that make him wake up cranky and reluctant to face the day. If his bedtime routine is not providing him with the night's sleep that he needs, Malki could plan a way to improve it. There may be habits she could instill that would help him feel more comfortable in school. If he has trouble sitting and focusing, she might be able to provide incentives, in cooperation with the teacher, to help him adjust to the more structured schedule.

Certainly, she needs to train him to wake up and get dressed without a fuss. While she did indeed have to meet the immediate challenge of getting him off to school that day, the best, farthest-reaching strategy would be to train him to go through the morning routine cooperatively. Then, the Level 2 immediate challenge would not even arise.

Obviously, the strategy she used of scolding and leaving her son feeling insulted did not qualify as training him to get up and dressed in a timely way. If she analyzed her situation according to the Five Level system, she would have realized that a change in Shimmy's behavior would require a structured plan carried out over time. She would not expect her lecture on Monday night to effect a change in his behavior on Tuesday.

Of course, not all goals can be adjourned for some time in the future. In Malki's case, a short-term, Level 2 strategy was also needed to get Shimmy out the door on time that morning. In a case where a child's health and well-being are at stake, an urgent response is needed. Even if a parent is working on training his toddler to touch his infant brother gently, the parent has to use a harsher, Level 1 response if the infant is in imminent danger.

Level 4: The Spiritual Side

As Jewish parents, we know that our responsibilities do not end at raising healthy children who possess the skills to live productive lives. We need to also help them internalize spiritual values: love and fear of Hashem, trust and faith in Him and a love of Torah and mitzvos.

This is perhaps our most delicate task. Not only are we responsible to train and inspire our children in these matters, but we must do so with the utmost care so that they never come to associate spirituality with feelings of rejection or hostility.

As we all know, being a *frum* Jew is a source of joy and satisfaction. The Torah affords us with all the guidelines needed for a fulfilling, happy life. At the same time, Judaism is not only about feeling good. Guiding children into Jewish adulthood requires teaching skills, such as reading Hebrew, *davening* and learning, as well as practices, such as attending *minyan* and saying *berachos*. Jewish observance also demands a great deal of restraint, which is anathema to most children. Getting them to do and say the right things is vital, and yet, if we accomplish this in a way that loses their hearts, we have lost everything.

Level 4 applies to many of the loftier, more subtle and long-term goals we have for our children. These include:

- Processing disappointments with acceptance;
- Facing fears with trust in Hashem;
- Seeing Hashem's hand in life's events;
- Reinforcing awareness of Hashem's gifts and kindness;
- Appreciating Shabbos;

- Delighting in the special flavor of each Yom Tov;
- Developing a love of mitzvos;
- Identifying with the Jewish people;
- Identifying with worthy role models;
- Nurturing a strong, positive feeling for a Torah-observant lifestyle

Our goals in Level 4 are united by their internal nature. Behavioral techniques are not enough. We can teach a child the right way to shake a *lulav*, but even his perfect performance is no indication of what is going on in his heart as he does the mitzvah. He will come to love this particular mitzvah if he comes to love the sights, aromas and sounds of *Succos*. He will love it if he feels his father's love for it; if he has the privilege of seeing a great rabbi perform the mitzvah with devotion; if he hears stories of *mesiras nefesh* for it; if he comprehends, on some level, the meaning of it.

Similarly, we are not likely to teach a child acceptance of Hashem's will by negating his disappointment and responding, "It's all for the best." Internalizing this concept takes many years of role-modeling, talking, helping a child to process negativity and finding the good in life's situations. In fact, it's a lifelong challenge.

Clearly, Level 4 goals are no place for a Level 1 reaction. We can't yell and *potch* our children into spiritual growth. To forestall immediate challenges (getting the non-kosher candy out of the child's hand) or to build long-term habits (getting to shul on time) Levels 2 and 3 methods can be useful. To move the heart, however, inspiration, teaching and positive experiences are the only effective ways.

Returning again to Malki and Shimmy, we see one dangerous pitfall emerging from the situation. Malki frames the situation at least partly as a Level 4 challenge. She elevates Shimmy's misbehavior to a transgression of *kibbud av v'eim* (the Fifth Commandment: honoring parents). Then she becomes a holy warrior, fighting not only to get her son to school on time, but to teach him that he cannot get away with defying Hashem.

Here Malki makes two errors. First of all, she has misidentified her goal. *Kibbud av v'eim* has little to do with the situation. The child is not defying G-d; he's having adjustment difficulties. Secondly, if she were sincerely trying to foster in her son a stronger feeling for this mitzvah, she has chosen the wrong tool. Her harsh reaction can only have the opposite effect. Perhaps the most spiritually destructive mistake a parent can make is to identify his own emotional outburst as religious zeal.

Level 5: A Healthy Heart

Parenting is the most altruistic work in existence. We pour everything we have into our children, all with the goal that they will sail forth in life, leave our homes, build their own families and carry on when we're gone. We build them not to keep them, but so that they can build others.

Level 5 is where we do this construction work. If a child were a house, he would need a strong frame to hold himself straight and solid against the winds. He would need a good roof so that negativity from the world around him could roll off and leave his interior intact. He would need plenty of doors, both to let others in and to secure himself against unwanted influences.

Finally, he would need a good heating and cooling system to generate warmth against a cold world, and to cool things down when emotions boil over. Translated into goals, Level 5 is where we:

- Build a child's sense of dignity and worth;
- Teach him that he is lovable;
- Build his confidence;
- Foster the ability to trust others;
- Help him develop the ability to express love;
- Teach him to accept others' love.

Level 5 goals encompass all the other levels as well. They refer to the emotional message that comes across with all our other responses. For example, a father may see his child running to chase a ball into the street. The father screams, "Get out of the street!" — an appropriate Level 1 response. For one child, the underlying message is, "I'm stupid. I did the wrong thing." For another child, the underlying message is "My father loves me. He's so scared that I'll be hurt!" While both children are startled and chastened, one child experiences an aftertaste of humiliation while the other experiences a sense of security.

What differentiates these children's experiences is the texture of their daily interactions with their parents. Often, we think of this "texture" as a natural outgrowth of our personality traits and innate people skills. We do not think of giving and receiving love as a "goal." We believe this ability stems from who we are rather than what we do. In reality, however, what we do can and does influence who we are.

Analyzing the Malki and Shimmy scenario in terms of Level 5 goals, we see that this is perhaps where the mother's response is the most counterproductive. Although she begins with the intention of appealing to her child's better self, her roiling tension takes over quickly. Her angry tone and labeling of Shimmy as a "lazy little boy" leave a little weak spot in the structure of the child she is "building."

Malki might say, "I can't help it. I have a temper. No matter how hard I try to keep a lid on it, eventually the pressure is too much and I explode. At least it blows over quickly." Nevertheless, she is building the framework upon which Shimmy's life will stand. A little rot on the center beam can spell trouble years later.

In Level 5, we will discover tools that parents can use, no matter what their natural personalities and traits, to reach the all-important goal of raising emotionally healthy children. This is where we hone the skills to raise a generation of loving, supportive spouses, good parents, trusted friends and cherished members of Klal Yisrael.

Using Your Tools

The coming chapters will guide you through the process of applying Five-Level Parenting to your life. We will first explore the specific challenges that face your family and your children. Then we will learn how to sort these challenges into the correct levels. Finally, we will learn about tools that you can use to meet each challenge in an effective, appropriate way. Throughout, you'll hear from parents who have used this method and found the sense of calm and accomplishment that comes from purposeful parenting. Here is where the real work begins.

Your Family

Can Five-Level Parenting work for your family? It can — provided you can step back from the day-to-day tumult and accurately identify the goals you have for each of your children. In this chapter, you'll be asked to focus on each of your children individually and assess the challenges he or she presents. Then you'll have a chance to think a little deeper: Can this specific challenge be solved by finding a more effective immediate response? Is it something that requires long-term training or re-training? Are there emotional or spiritual issues attached to the challenge? Once you've mapped out your goals for your children, you will have designed your blueprint for progress.

Let's take an example to see how this process works.

Nussi and Ruchi are the parents of four children: Temima, 7 years old; Daniel, 5 years old; Gavriel, 3 years old, and Raizy, 1 year old. Ever since Raizy was born, the parents feel overwhelmed. They are torn between the demands of the small children and the need to establish order and routine for the school-age children. Homework time is constantly being interrupted by the little kids. The baby wants to be held and nursed frequently. If she is quiet enough for Ruchi to put her down, little Gavriel is soon on the scene trying to explore the baby's eyeballs. Ruchi rarely gets through Chumash review with her daughter and Daniel's alef-beis review is rarely even started.

Bedtime is a fruitless endeavor; the baby wakes up Gavriel and soon the whole house is awake, thirsty, in need of the bathroom, scared, too hot or too cold. Ruchi is up and down and back and forth all night long. Nussi tries to help, but the children invariably scream for their mother; it seems counterproductive to have Nussi struggle against resistance to do something Ruchi could do in a snap.

Besides the difficulties with daily routines, the parents seem unable to curtail the constant bickering and fighting between the two older kids. Daniel is a hot-tempered child who reacts to frustration by kicking and throwing things at his sister. Temima sees herself as the "little mother" and is constantly trying to boss Daniel around, which triggers his temper.

The fighting, unfortunately, seems to peak at the Shabbos table. The beautiful, warm family experience Ruchi and Nussi dreamed about as a newly married couple has turned into a chaotic ordeal that sometimes leaves Ruchi in tears.

Many parents of young families — maybe even most of them — would call this scenario a normal "day in the life." Ruchi and Nussi could just plow forward, secure in the knowledge that in about 25 years or so, they will probably regain some control of their lives. Instead, they decide to take matters in hand. They recognize that interrupted sleep, poor homework habits and fighting will not help their children build a foundation for success. They decide to try the Five-Level Parenting approach.

The first step in the process is to answer four questions:

1. What is the most immediate and important problem or problems you are facing right now?

2. What times of day and what situations are the most challenging?

3. List all your children aged 2-13. How would you want each of them to change?

4. Overall, how would you rate the difficulty you have with your children from 1-10 (10 being the most difficult)?

Let's put ourselves in Nussi's and Ruchi's shoes now, and see how they might assess their situation.

Question 1: The first question is the "triage" question that identifies the problems that need attention right away.

We need to get homework and bedtime under control. It's not fair to Temima and Daniel that I'm constantly being interrupted when I try to review with them. Daniel is only 5 and he's already falling behind. Temima goes to school unprepared and her teachers notice. And they're so tired in the morning. If we don't take care of this situation now, we're really worried that they will fall behind and begin to feel bad about themselves.

Question 2: The second question helps define the limits of the problem. Thoughts like "They're *always* fighting" or "They *never* listen" make our challenges seem infinite. We can end up feeling frustrated as if we are doomed to endlessly push a heavy boulder up a mountain. If we can identify a specifically difficult

time period, we can put the challenges in perspective and focus our efforts where they most are needed.

The answer to that one is simple: from 4 o'clock when the big kids come home from school until about 10 at night when everyone is usually finally asleep for the night.

Question 3: Here is where we begin sorting out the situation. Rather than thinking "the kids" are out of control, we focus on each one and what challenges he or she presents.

Temima: She is too dependent on me to get her started and keep her going on her homework. She needs to see it as her job and see me just as her helper. It would also help if she could be less bossy to Daniel.

Daniel: His short fuse disrupts everything. We want him to learn a little patience and self-control.

Gavriel: He doesn't stay in bed. As soon as Raizy starts crying, he wants to begin the whole night all over again. We want him to learn that even if he is awakened, he needs to stay in bed and go back to sleep. We also want him to accept his father as the one who sometimes does his bedtime routine or maybe answers him if he calls out at night.

Question 4: Rating the overall situation in terms of the level of difficulty gives us a basis of comparison as we move forward with the Five-Level method. By rating how difficult our situation was at first, we can accurately assess how much it has improved in the interim. This keeps us motivated and helps us stick with the program.

We know from talking to friends that our household isn't much different than many others. However, we feel that there's great room for improvement. We believe in an organized, efficient household because we know the kids will grow up much more secure and accomplished that way. We also know that we'll be happier and better parents if we can get certain things under control. So we'll rate our situation at around 7: not the worst, but definitely serious.

Sorting It All Out

Now that we have a picture of the challenges the parents are facing with their children and idea of how often, when and to what degree these challenges arise, we can begin sorting them into levels.

Level 1: Preventing disaster

Here is where we prepare to deal with situations that could potentially cause serious, irrevocable damage or injury. The best Level 1 response is one that comes before damage is actually done; while a child is in the midst of embarking on the dangerous act. If we can catch the child at that point and react with a strong, high-impact response, we can prevent the harm at the moment and most likely, forever thereafter.

Sometimes, however, parents do not know soon enough that damage is forthcoming. For instance, Ruchi may not have thought that Gavriel's "making nice" to the baby will, one second later, turn into a slap on the baby's head. If that happens, *a strong, Level 1 response will help to ensure that it never happens again.* Two of the challenges that Nussi and Ruchi listed above fall under this category:

1. Gavriel might touch the baby in a way that could seriously hurt her; he might poke her eye or do something far worse.

2. Daniel might pick up something heavy or sharp, like a wooden building block, and strike his sister in a way that would do serious damage.

Level 2: Avoiding "normal" damage at the moment

This is where we prepare effective responses and tools to change children's behavior in the moment when they are in the midst of doing something they must not do, or refusing to do something they must do. Unlike Level 1 situations, these challenges are not dangerous or life threatening. Goals that fall within this level include:

1. Stopping Gavriel as he disturbs the baby, even when his behavior doesn't pose a risk of danger;

2. Getting Temima to start her homework promptly and go back to it when her parents tell her to do so;

3. Stopping Temima as she provokes Daniel;

3. Stopping Daniel in his tracks as he starts to lose his temper;

4. Curtailing the bedtime disturbances as they erupt.

Level 3: Long-term training to eliminate improper behaviors and develop proper skills and habits

Level 3 is where we focus on training and routines. Many of the situations we address as immediate concerns in Level 2 can be addressed at the same time with a long-term approach in Level 3. Here's the difference: At Level 2, we aim our response at stopping or starting a behavior *in the moment*, while in Level 3, our goal is to *train* the child to change the behavior. For Ruchi and Nussi, Level 3 goals are:

1. Training Gavriel not to touch the baby;

2. Training Temima and Daniel to begin their homework on time and stay on task until it is finished, even in the face of distractions;

3. Training Temima not to provoke Daniel;

4. Training Daniel to react calmly to provocations;

5. Training the children to adhere to a bedtime routine;

6. Training the children to stay in bed at night, and to only come out for emergencies;

7. Training the children to obey their parents' directives;

8. Training all the children, but especially Gavriel, to respond to Nussi as a caregiver so that Ruchi can have backup when needed.

Level 4: Instilling important values in the child

At this level, we concentrate on imparting to our children the values we hold to be important in life. This includes virtues such as helpfulness, compassion, personal responsibility and a balanced view of materialism vs. spirituality, the proper way to relate to others, their relationship to Hashem and the Jewish people, their ethics and integrity.

1. For Temima, personal responsibility. She doesn't seem to feel any obligation to get her homework done or to put away her belongings or help with household chores. If no one is on top of her, she lets things slide.

2. Making Shabbos into an eagerly anticipated, special day for all the children.

3. Improving the children's *kibbud av v'eim.*

Level 5: Helping the child learn to process emotions, feel loved and be emotionally healthy

This is the level at which we tend to the child's self-esteem, emotional awareness and communication skills. Our goal is to impart a secure feeling within him that he is a valuable person who is worthy of others' love and respect and able to give love and respect to others.

1. Dealing with Daniel's anger and helping him to deal with his siblings peacefully.

2. Channeling Temima's "mothering" instinct into something appropriate for her age so that she can relate normally to siblings and friends.

3. Creating an atmosphere in which the children feel that the parents are happy to be with them rather than that they are overwhelmed.

4. Defining limits and maintaining routines so the children will develop a sense of security and responsibility.

As we see, many goals spill over into a few categories. For instance, the couple identifies one Level 5 goal as "Creating an atmosphere in which the children feel that the parents are happy to be with them rather than that they are overwhelmed." At Level 1, the end to Gavriel's assaults on the baby and Daniel's physical attacks on his sister will certainly take some of the tension out of the air. At Level 2, getting the children to comply with routines will no doubt lessen the parents' frustration level. When they accomplish Level 3 training, the entire household will be functioning more smoothly and everyone will be getting the sleep they need. At Level 4, the children will gradually learn to heed their parents and at times even enjoy it, because it is a mitzvah to do so. At Level 5, the parents will actually work directly on building a positive bond with their children, but the other four levels will help make that work much easier and more effective.

One of the greatest sources of parental frustration comes from confusion between Level 2 and Level 3. Effective short-term interventions, while essential, are not a replacement for long-term training. Level 2 is like the treatment of an illness, for instance, a few doses of cough syrup for a cold. Level 3 is a proactive, preventive measure, like increasing the child's intake of fruits and vegetables so that he does not come down with colds. Obviously, the parent has to respond to the child's immediate symptom, but if day after day, week after week, the child is continually coming down with a cold, the cough syrup is obviously not making life better for the child or the parent.

In the same way, Level 2 interventions must be used as situations arise, but they cannot be the end of the story. These tools are not meant to be a daily or hourly occurrence. For instance, a child cannot spend hours each day in time-out. Parents sometimes believe they are "training" their children to stop a negative behavior through Level 2 tools such as time-out, and they become desperate when their "training" doesn't seem to solve the problem. The answer to their frustration resides in Level 3. They need an actual training plan, not just a response. They need to back up their immediate response with a program that eradicates the negative behavior and instills a positive behavior in its place. As the Level 3 plan begins to work, the parents will find that they need their Level 2 tools far less often.

As you look at Nussi and Ruchi's list, you might see it as a dauntingly long agenda of items and issues. However, many of these challenges can be fixed relatively quickly and very efficiently with tools that are simple to use. Many parents imagine that the children's negative behaviors are complex and intractable, requiring the parenting-skill equivalent of brain surgery, when in fact, the challenges respond perfectly well to the equivalent of an aspirin. It won't take long for the family to achieve a significant change.

Now that you have seen how to define and sort various parenting challenges, it's time to apply this method to your own family. Keep in mind that you, as the parents, are the ones who can best determine the right goals for your children. The system will not work if you choose goals that are too far above or below your children at this point in their lives. As you learn to use this method and experience success, you and your family can reach higher together.

Please use the space below to answer the four questions we reviewed in this chapter.

1. What is the most immediate and important problem or problems you are facing right now? _____

_____

_____

_____

_____

2. What times of day and what situations are the most challenging? _____

_____

_____

3. List all your children that are ages 2-13. How would you want each of them to change? _____

_____

_____

_____

_____

_____

_____

_____

_____

_____

4. Overall, how would you rate the difficulty you have with your children from 1-10 (10 being the most difficult)? _____

In the space below, sort the goals you described for your children into the appropriate levels. You do not need to elaborate; just state the goal clearly enough for your own use. If you are dealing with a complex situation in which there are many children and/or many challenges, use your answer to Question 1 to focus your attention on your immediate priorities. What changes would make the biggest difference for your family? Start there; when you see improvement in that area, you can reassess and see what needs to be done next. You might even find out that lesser challenges fade as the larger ones are overcome.

Level 1: Emergency intervention to prevent irrevocable disaster

Level 2: Immediate intervention to prevent "normal" damage at the moment

Level 3: Long-term training to eliminate improper behaviors and develop proper skills and habits

Level 4: Instilling important values in the child

Level 5: Helping the child learn to process emotions, feel loved and be emotionally healthy

You have now created a road map. You know where you wish to go with each of your children. You have identified your vision of a successful family life, and the obstacles that currently stand in the way of turning that vision into reality.

Our next important step is to learn how to overcome those obstacles. This we will do by using a full toolbox of proven parenting methods. In each of the coming chapters, we'll discuss the tools available for each level of challenge and how to use them effectively. We'll hear from parents who have used these tools successfully to bring harmony and happiness into their homes. Then we'll stop reading and start moving toward the family and home we want and *can have.*

Part 2:
The Five Levels

Level 1: For Emergency Use Only

In Level 1 our goal is to avoid significant irrevocable harm. We will use these tools:

- *Establishing Safety*
- *Instilling Fear*

Shlomo HaMelech teaches (*Koheles* 3:1-8) that there is a proper time for everything: birth and death, building and destroying, rejoicing and mourning, war and peace. Obviously, in all of these matters, the pleasant way is preferable. For instance, we desire peace and pursue it at every opportunity, but there is also a time for war. If we are not willing to wage war when necessary, we cannot protect ourselves from evil and aggression. Nonetheless, no sane person would propose that war is the first or best answer to every adversarial encounter.

This paradigm illustrates the rightful place of harsh parenting methods such as *potching* and yelling. They are the "war" option that we seek to avoid at all costs. However, like war, these methods have their place, and that is when peaceful options would leave the child vulnerable to serious, irrevocable harm.

Level 1 tools seem quite simple — even instinctive. After all, what parent has not had the urge to yell or *potch* a stubborn, unruly child? The wisdom we need to acquire in Level 1 is not so much *what* to do, but *when* and *in what spirit* we must do it. Let's first look at the simplest question: What specific tools are effective for Level 1 challenges?

Establishing Safety

At Level 1, you are faced with a situation in which something tragic and/or irreversible might happen if the child's action is not stopped immediately. Most of these situations involve young children who are not yet able to assess risks and dangers. When you are dealing with small children, you usually have the ability to step in and physically remove the child from danger. Some tools to establish safety include:

• Lifting the child up and moving him out of harm's way

A toddler is walking too close to the edge of a swimming pool. If the mother calls to him from her seat, he might not hear her or he might be thrown off balance and fall in. If she fears he is at risk of falling in, she needs to get up and physically remove him from the dangerous area.

• Confining the child to an area where he has no access to a potential danger

A family is having a barbecue in a park. Their 2-year-old is fascinated by the flames, which are at his eye level and are occasionally flaring in the breeze. As he reaches toward the fire, his mother scoops him up and secures him in his stroller. Although the child is struggling and crying, the mother knows that if she simply removes the child, his curiosity will lead him right back to the fire. She also knows that she is watching four other children and might not notice what he is doing. Therefore, to establish safety, she must put the little boy someplace where it will be impossible for him to reach the fire.

- Taking the danger away from the child

A 4-year-old girl decides to make herself a snack as she has seen her mother do. She takes an apple from the refrigerator and takes her mother's sharp knife out of the drawer. Just as she is about to start chopping, her mother walks in and sees her. If the mother first yells, "No! Rivky! Put that knife down!" the little girl could be startled and cut herself. The mother establishes safety by moving swiftly to remove the knife from the child's grasp.

- Preventing the child from harming others

An 8-year-old boy is walking to the store with his mother and his baby brother, who is in a carriage. The boy asks to wheel the carriage and the mother allows him to do so. The boy starts zigzagging and running heedlessly with the carriage. The mother runs to catch up and grabs hold of the carriage.

Had she called to the boy, he might not have heard, or may have heard too late. Had she caught up with him and merely lectured him about being irresponsible with the carriage, he might have calmed down for a few minutes and then resumed his games. She could not take a chance on the baby being hurt, and so, she removed the baby from the boy.

- Yelling

A 10-year-old is in a hurry to get on his bike and ride with his friends to the park where a softball game will take place. He can't find his helmet and has no patience to look for it. As he rides out of his driveway, his father notices him from his bedroom window. By the time the father would get downstairs to the front door to stop his son, the boy would be gone. The father opens the window and yells, "Yaakov! Off that bike now! Get into the house!"

Instilling Fear

Once the child is out of danger, there is another Level 1 goal to achieve. That is to make sure that the child never again engages in the dangerous activity. Although generally we do not want to alarm our children or traumatize them, in this one narrow area, a measure of alarm is necessary. Children have to experience these dangers as outside the realm of acceptable. You want to do everything you can to ensure that even if you turn your back or have a lapse in supervision, your child will not go beyond certain boundaries.

The fear we are seeking to produce is not fear of your wrath, but rather, fear of the dangerous activity. Since small children cannot perceive such dangers, we have to create in them a distinctly negative association with that activity. In older children, we may be able to use strong, stark words to instill that fear.

You will have far more success accomplishing your goals if your interactions with your children are usually calm. Then when you respond with some fire and passion, they will perceive very clearly that this situation is different.

There are only a few tools for instilling fear. These include:

- A *potch* and a sharp scolding

Levi moves to a large housing development. His house faces a much traveled street, and he knows it will be a challenge to prevent his curious, active 2-year-old from stepping off the curb.

Soon after the family moves in, Levi takes his son outside and follows him around as he wanders. He tells the child several times to stay on the sidewalk, and shows him exactly where he is not permitted to go. Soon enough, however, the child nears the edge of the curb, looks around and begins stepping into forbidden territory. Levi is there in a flash. He grabs him firmly, pulls him back onto the curb, gives him one sharp potch and yells, "No! You must never, never walk into the street! You can get very, very hurt. Never do that again!"

The boy is shocked at his father's reaction. He cries hard. Levi picks him up and begins to soothe him. He can revert to the normal affectionate relationship now because the harsh response has achieved its purpose. In the child's mind, the act of stepping into the street is now firmly associated with pain. Although the parents still need to remain vigilant, the child never steps off the curb again.

- Verbal "shock and awe"

It's time to light Chanukah candles. One of the children, a 6-year-old, picks up the box of matches and begins trying to strike one. The father quickly removes the matches from the child's hands. "Do you know what can happen if you play with matches? You can start a fire. It can be a tiny little fire that no one even notices, but it can spread and the house can burn down. We can all chas v'shalom be very hurt or even die." For the rest of Chanukah, the child stayed far from the matches.

The tools for Level 1 may seem harsh, and in fact they are. That is because they are emergency measures, life- and limb-saving interventions when nothing else will do. Not using them when they are needed is far more dangerous to a child and a family — sometimes irreversibly so — than dealing with the tears and fears these measures may evoke.

The Right Time, the Right Situation

For some parents, the Level 1 tools named above are not reserved for emergencies. Rather, they are the bread and butter of their parenting interactions. Hitting, yelling and harshness are the default mode for those who:

- Have a short temper and little tolerance for children;
- Don't know what else to do when children won't obey;
- Sincerely believe that this is the most effective way to assert authority over a child;
- Were raised with such a parenting style and use that as their model.

However, as we noted earlier, Level 1 responses are most effective for parents who use them only infrequently. A parent who is always yelling and hitting desensitizes his children to these reactions. Instead of thinking, *Wow! This must be something really serious to get my father so upset!* the child thinks, *There he goes again, turning everything into a drama.* The child will fail to distinguish between dangerous infractions and those that simply annoy his parents.

In addition, parents who constantly issue dire warnings about things that are fairly benign will not be heard when their warnings pertain to something truly dangerous.

"If you go out in the rain without your boots, you can catch pneumonia and end up in the hospital like Uncle Aaron."

"Put down that baseball! You can fracture someone's skull with that!"

"No roller-skating for you. I'm not having you spend the winter in a cast like your cousin Rena did."

If parents present puddles, baseballs and roller skates as mortal threats, they should not be surprised when in later years, their children don't hear their warnings about cigarettes, careless driving or even unsavory friends. The "shock and awe" approach fails to shock or awe if it becomes business as usual.

Overusing drastic measures not only robs them of their impact, but also, it almost always fails to solve the issue. Hitting and yelling about homework will not train the child to build good study habits. If anything, these responses will make the task even more abhorrent. Neither will this approach instill *kibbud av v'eim.* The child might fear his parents' outbursts, but he will soon perceive that he is witnessing a loss of self-control rather than an expression of true authority. His respect for his parents will be diminished rather than elevated.

Therefore, before sliding into a Level 1 response, you will want to be very sure that it is really the right tool for the situation. If you are the type of person who might naturally lapse into yelling or hitting, force yourself to answer a short, self-administered questionnaire before you decide that your response is the right one for the situation. Ask yourself:

1. Is anyone about to be injured seriously if this activity repeats or continues?

2. Is this a real tragedy waiting to happen, or am I simply very annoyed or inconvenienced by this behavior?

Asking yourself these questions helps you to make a correct snap decision about using a Level 1 tool. Given the emergency nature of these situations, snap decisions are your only option.

Even if you do determine that Level 1 is the appropriate response for a situation, you cannot use it over and over again for the same challenge. We don't want to be in the position of having to escalate our response every time a child re-tests the limits. Therefore, it is wise to support Level 1 responses with reinforcement from Levels 3, 4 and 5. In other words, Levi's little boy in the story above should be trained at Level 3, through reinforcement and rewards, to stay on the sidewalk; he should learn on Level 4 the value of taking care of his body, health and safety, and he should learn on Level 5 that his parents' strictness about this rule comes from their deep love for him.

The Right Spirit

Level 1 presents a dilemma in that yelling, *potching* and allowing harsh consequences to take place do not feel like love to our children. We are doing to them what they do to each other when they get frustrated and their tempers flare. So how do we let them know that we're not just big kids having a fight with them and winning because we're so much bigger?

That message comes through to them clearly if the message is true. If there is anger, irritation, arrogance or frustration in our response, our children will perceive it immediately. Only when we grab the reins of our emotions and move with purpose, solely for the sake of protecting our beloved children from harm, are we able to pack our response with the gravity it deserves. When we know we're in control, they know it too.

Equally important is the context of the rest of our relationship with our children. Imagine that a father brings his little daughter to the doctor for an injection. She's scared. She's crying. Worse yet, it's her father — the one she counts on to protect her — who is restraining her so the nurse can hit her target. Nevertheless, the little girl doesn't feel betrayed; she is still sure of her father's love because he shows it every day in every way possible. Likewise, when a harsh reaction is an infrequent anomaly in the parent-child relationship, the children's faith in their parents' love is not shaken.

From *Kayin's* strike against *Hevel* to *Moshe Rabbeinu's* ill-fated striking of the rock, our Torah lays out the dire consequences of acting out of anger. Nothing in this chapter should be seen as condoning anger or justifying it in certain circumstances.

As a therapist, I cannot stress enough the far-reaching repercussions of angry parenting. I work with many clients who grew up under this cloud and need a great deal of healing. They often struggle with anxiety, depression, low self-esteem and many other debilitating mental health issues. Often times, they end up having to struggle with a terrible temper of their very own. When they don't seek help, the pain they harbor inside seeps into every corner of their lives, damaging their marriages and their children.

Nevertheless, as we conveyed earlier, there is a time for everything, including harshness. By learning how and when to use a Level 1 response, you have a powerful, essential tool for averting the types of tragedies from which we all pray to be protected. My hope is that you'll be able to keep this tool tucked away unused, and guide your children, safe and sound, through childhood's many unpredictable moments.

Your Level 1

In the space below, list the challenges you named in the previous chapter that fall under the category of Level 1. Next to each challenge, name the tools you will use to "establish safety" and "instill fear."

Situation	Tools

Level 2: The Here and Now

In Level 2 our goal is to avoid "normal" damage at the moment. We will use these tools:

- *Doing Nothing*
- *Taking Action*
- *1-2-3*
- *Using "Stations"*
- *Establishing Family Rules*
- *Pre-setting Behaviors*

When a child touches a hot stove, he removes his hand immediately and never touches the stove again. Why does he not try it a second or third time to see if perhaps this time, he can touch the hot stove without getting burned? The reason is that he has learned a lesson: fire burns. His parents don't have to say a word about it. He perceives that this is an inviolable law of nature that will operate the same way every time.

We see another illustration of this principle when we take a child shopping with us at a non-Jewish supermarket. He may ask for the candies and chocolates he sees at the check-out counter, but when we tell him, "It's not kosher," there is rarely an argument. He knows there will never be a time when we "just this once" let him eat a non-kosher item.

The consistency of the outcome is what keeps the child from trying to negotiate another chance to touch the flame or permission to have the non-kosher candy. Similarly Level 2 is about creating consistent consequences that stop a behavior immediately. It creates a "cause and effect" relationship between certain actions and certain results, and it does so without any need to resort to lectures or high emotions. A child learns that "If I play with my glass, it will be taken away" not because "I made Mommy angry" but because "That's what happens when I play with my glass."

By learning and using these methods for appropriate situations, parents take themselves out of the frustrating cycle of repeated warnings and punishments followed by repeated misbehaviors. Often these situations are not really cycles, but spirals, because as the parent is forced to repeat himself over and over again, he becomes angrier, sometimes ending in hitting, yelling or shaming the child.

Used correctly, Level 2 methods create a consistent reality for a child that stops him from behaving in an inappropriate or destructive way. They are tools for the here and now, when a parent's mind is screaming, *This must not happen!* Often, Level 3 tools are needed to help a child form better habits over the long term, but many behaviors first demand an immediate, effective response.

Level 2 applies to ordinary situations that do not present Level 1, potentially disastrous results. It can apply to one-time situations such as being quiet during a speech at a *simchah* or behaving on a long car ride; to routines like getting up, eating meals, bedtime and doing homework; and to behavior issues like fighting, grabbing toys, yelling, kvetching, wildness and speaking disrespectfully. When we want something to happen *now* or stop *now*, Level 2 tools are the ones we need. Let's examine these tools and see how they operate.

Doing Nothing

For a parent with a healthy dose of patience and at least a dim memory of what it feels like to be a child, this tool is easy to access. There's a certain amount of leeway we can and should allow so that we are not constantly interfering with our children's autonomy. If they are not hurting anyone, hurting themselves, creating a nuisance or a danger, then the best strategy is to let them "do their thing."

Ari comes home from yeshivah with a bag full of candy, cookies and chips left over from his class siyum. He is halfway through the bag by the time he steps off the bus, and as soon as he gets home, he digs in to finish the job. As he tells his mother about the great siyum, which included keyboard music by the rebbi, plus hot potato kugel prepared by his classmate's mother, he continues to chomp on the contents of his bag.

His mother's stomach is practically churning as she watches this nutritional nightmare. However, Ari is an active boy with a healthy appetite. He rarely indulges in such mounds of nosh, and he is clearly enjoying it now. The mother's first impulse is to say, "I think that's enough nosh for now." But instead, she keeps quiet, knowing that when he's full, he'll stop, and even if he loses his appetite for dinner this evening, it won't be the end of the world.

Doing nothing can also take the form of a parent's firm resolve to ignore a child's demands. For instance, if a child is sitting in front of a perfectly acceptable plate of food — food he has eaten many times — but insisting that his dinner must consist of Honey Nut Cheerios this evening, his mother can handle the situation by doing nothing. She doesn't try to force him to eat what she prepared, but neither does she accede to the demands of her demanding little customer. She simply tells him, "This is what we have for supper. You can have Cheerios for breakfast." Even if the child goes without dinner, the situation will not present a Level 1 danger; the mother can do nothing and the child will not starve.

Similarly, some parents use "doing nothing" as the response to a messy bedroom. When a child is old enough to care for his or her own clothing and living space, but shows great resistance to doing so, the situation can spawn endless battles. Sometimes, once the child is drowning in dirty laundry and can't find more than one of any given pair of shoes, he develops an internal motivation for some modicum of orderliness. He might not become Mr. Neat, but he will at least understand that no one is going to save him from the consequences of his messiness.

Taking Action

Many Level 2 situations do not lend themselves to doing nothing. When children are flinging their food across the table or throwing a tantrum in the ice-cream aisle of the grocery store, ignoring the behavior is not an option. Sometimes the simplest and most effective means to regain control of the runaway train is to pull the emergency brake: make the situation grind to a halt instantaneously.

Taking action comes in two forms: Calmly removing the child from the situation or calmly removing the situation from the child.

- *Five-year-old Rivky is fascinated by the ceramic candy dish on her grandmother's coffee table. She picks it up and begins walking away with it. Her mother says, "Rivky, that's Bubbi's special dish and it can break if it drops. Please put it down." Rivky keeps her hold on it and begins to argue. Her mother takes action to stop the situation from going any further. She takes the dish from Rivky and places it on a high shelf. (She removes the situation from the child.)*

- *Four-year-old Shaindy and 7-year-old Shmuelly are sitting on the couch one Friday night after they've finished eating. The rest of the family is still at the table in the adjacent dining room. Although the couch seats four adults comfortably, Shaindy has pushed herself right up against Shmuelly. "You're squishing me!" Shmuelly complains. The father tells Shaindy to move over and give her brother some space. Shaindy complies, but a few seconds later, Shmuelly is heard whining, "Get your feet off me!" The father sees that from her new spot a few feet from Shmuelly, Shaindy has extended her leg to poke him in the thigh. Clearly, the cycle is not going to stop. The father now takes action. He lifts Shaindy from the couch and seats her on the armchair. "You have this seat and Shmuelly has that one." (He removes the child from the situation.)*

- *Nine-year-old Boruch is talented with his hands. He is permitted to use his father's tools for his many projects. However, despite reminders and discussions about responsibility, Boruch often forgets to put the tools away. One rainy afternoon, the father catches sight of his hammer and his ratchet set sitting in a puddle in the yard. He takes action. He brings the tools in, dries them off and places them in his locked tool cabinet. The next time Boruch needs the tools, he cannot find them. He asks his father where they were and his father replies, "I put them away until you're old enough to take proper care of them." (He removes the situation from the child.)*

- *Leah and Naomi, two 11-year-old cousins, sit together in shul at Leah's brother's bar mitzvah. Naomi has come from out of town for the occasion and the two girls are giddy with the pleasure of being together. They continually whisper to each other while the Torah reading is going on. Leah's mother turns and "shushes" them. In moments, their whispering resumes. The mother "shushes" them again, now a bit angrily. The next time she hears their voices, just a few moments later, she walks to where they are sitting and motions for her daughter to move over one seat. The mother sits down in between the girls. (She does a combination of removing the child from the situation and the situation from the child.)*

The common thread in the actions these parents took was that Doing Nothing was not an option. When that is the case, Taking Action is the next best strategy. Had the parents not taken action, we can be 110 percent certain that the situations would have escalated beyond reason. The children's provocations would have continued as the parents' growing sense of helplessness turned to anger. Relatively benign instances of annoying behavior would have caused a disproportionate eruption of emotion.

- Rivky's mother would have repeated her warnings again and again, louder and more adamant each time, until she either screamed at the child or the child broke the candy dish and the mother screamed even louder.
- Shaindy would have continued provoking her brother until her father either screamed in frustration at the constant irritation, or got up and gave her a *potch*.
- Boruch's father might have continued lecturing his son on responsibility, all to no avail, until the tools were ruined and he felt he had to punish Boruch.
- Leah's mother would have shushed the girls a dozen more times, getting angrier and angrier, clouding the family's *simchah* with negative emotions all around.

One of the major obstacles parents have to taking action is that it requires more energy and effort than is required for warning and yelling while seated in place. Since most parents work hard and sleep too little, they have a resistance to jumping up to take action where words would seem to be enough. Often, mothers have another child on their hands or in their hands, and can't necessarily rush to take action.

However, in most cases, it's possible, for instance, to put a baby down in an infant seat or place a task on hold for a moment to "take action" when action is needed. The effort is worthwhile because by taking action, parents can solve a lingering, annoying situation in an instant, without anger. The firm, calm approach is what gives this method its effectiveness; no matter how loudly the child objects to the parent's action, the parent simply goes ahead. The message to the child is, "This is what happens when you…." There is no basis for argument or negotiations.

Taking Action is a Level 2 tool, but it sometimes has a Level 3 training value as well. It helps children internalize the idea that there are limits which their parents will not allow them to cross. Parents who don't take action often say, "My kids only listen when I yell." That is because they have taught their children unwittingly that they need not respond to the parents' words. Mommy will just keep asking — once, twice, six times, ten times — and when she really means it, she will yell. But when a child knows that his parents will take action, he has no benefit in persisting in the activity.

One, Two, Three, Time-Out

"Time-out" has become a staple in the modern parenting tool-box. The goal is simple: It's a way to calmly stop the child in his or her tracks without the parent needing to take further action. Once the child has experienced the consistent use of proper time-out technique a few times, it becomes an incredibly effective tool. Even when it doesn't work to stop the child, it still operates as a form of Taking Action by removing the child from the situation.

The technique is very simple: A child is behaving in an unacceptable way. The parent directs him to stop. The child persists in the behavior. At that point, the parent begins counting to three out loud: "That's one … that's two … that's three … time-out."

While the parent is counting, the child still has the opportunity to stop the behavior. Once the count is finished, the child must go to a specified time-out location and remain there for a set period. Most parenting experts recommend one minute for each year of the child's age. For example, a 3-year-old would have to stay in time-out for three minutes.

An important element of this technique is the parent's demeanor of firm, calm control over the situation. Lecturing and scolding are counterproductive. The child must understand only that he has been asked to stop a negative behavior and has chosen to continue it instead. Therefore, the parent is taking the initiative to put an end to the behavior. How, why and who's to blame are irrelevant.

The main benefit of this technique is that it tells the child instantly that there will be no ongoing struggle over the issue at hand. He will either stop his behavior on his own within the next three seconds, or he will be forced to stop it. Knowing this gives him the motivation to rein in his unacceptable behavior on his own; he realizes that he will not have the opportunity to win a battle of wills.

From the parent's point of view, this technique provides a sense of calm: No matter how disruptive or irritating the child's behavior, there is an end in sight. The desperate feeling of "How can I make this *stop*?" dissipates, and with that, the rising adrenalin dissipates as well. The beauty of time-out is that it eliminates long negotiations and arguments, and stops the negative behavior rather than allowing it to go another round and then another. There's a light at the end of the tunnel, and the tunnel is only three seconds long.

We should mention, however, that time-out can be misused to the detriment of the child's emotional growth. In their landmark parenting book, *How to Talk So Kids Will Listen and Listen So Kids Will Talk* (re-published by Scribner, 2012), authors Adele Faber and Elaine Mazlish warn that children's aggressive behavior often arises from provocation by a friend or sibling, and time-out in that case will only leave them feeling angrier at the injustice they've been dealt.

Many parents find, however, that talking to the child about other ways to handle an underlying problem is not enough to curtail the behavior. Instead, the parent might find himself having to take action over and over again as the child keeps going back into the fray. While changing that behavior over the long term might require Level 3 training, time-out provides a non-negotiable limit to the child's immediate behavior.

Let's assume, for instance, that 5-year-old Moshe has a 3-year-old sister, Rivky, who loves to interfere when he plays with his building blocks. His mother has already discussed his grievances and helped him find alternatives to hitting his sister. He knows, "I'm not allowed to hit Rivky, even if she knocks over my blocks. Instead, I could give her some blocks to play with herself. Or I could play with something else and save blocks for when she's napping. Or I could play blocks in my room with the door closed. Or I can ask Mommy to help me."

One day, he takes out his blocks. He wants to play with them now, not when Rivky naps. He wants to play with them in the living room, near his mother, not alone in his bedroom. Predictably, Rivky is on the scene in seconds. Mom is close by in the kitchen, but she can't see the children. Little Moshe has a big temper, and the very sight of his sister approaching with mischievous glee in her eyes drives all his more civilized responses out his head. He screams, "No! Rivky, no!" and tackles her. By the time Mom rushes in to investigate the commotion, Rivky is crying bitter tears and a red-faced Moshe is sitting on her chubby little legs trying to prevent her from reaching the blocks.

"Get off Rivky, Moshe. Right now," Mom demands. Moshe is in a frenzy. He's not budging. "One —," Mom starts counting. "Two —" Moshe looks calmer. He's considering his options. "Three —" Moshe digs in. He can't bring himself to surrender. "Time-out, Moshe," Mom states firmly. She takes his hand and leads him to a chair in the den. She shows him on the clock when five minutes will be over and leaves the room. She hasn't yelled; she hasn't lectured Moshe about hurting people or loving his siblings; she hasn't called him a name like "bully" or "bad boy." She hasn't spurred him to raise one defense or argument. He knew what was coming and it came.

It may be true that Moshe feels unjustly punished for a situation that, in his view, is all Rivky's fault. However, he also knows that physical aggression is not allowed in his family, and that he has crossed that boundary. His mother has demonstrated to him that this boundary is real and will be defended. On a deeper level, this can help him feel secure and regain his composure.

To use time-out effectively, parents need to prepare their response. They should choose a place for the child to sit and let the children know in advance how the system will work. For young children who might not grasp an explanation, it's sufficient to warn them as the behavior occurs: "I'm going to count to three now and give you a chance to stop, but if you don't, then you have to go to time-out. One — two — three —"

Since children do not always docilely follow their parents' directions to go to time-out, parents need to develop a backup strategy. What happens if the child will not go? What happens if the child will not stay?

The most common response parents come up with in these situations is to physically put the child where he needs to be. If the child is small enough, lift him up and place him in his time-out location. A room with a door is best for children who may not comply on their own, because in that case, many parents find that they must hold the door shut for the few minutes the child is in time-out.

Children may try to escalate the situation by saying disrespectful things or throwing tantrums in protest against their parents' discipline, thus adding a lot of fire and fury to a method designed to be gentle. Parents should ignore the theatrics as much as possible, concentrating on the issue that prompted the time-out, and on getting the child to spend those few minutes alone, away from the situation that sparked his misbehavior. Often, once children realize that the parents are serious about enforcing time-out, they will stop objecting and use the time as it is meant to be used: to experience a firm end-point for a negative behavior.

Using Stations

Eli and Chaya were two years apart, as close as two siblings could be. They had a crazy energy together, fueled by an entire repertoire of private jokes and funny faces that no one else in the family understood.

When they were small, their antics brought smiles from their parents and siblings. But as they reached what everyone thought ought to be the age of reason — Eli was 8 and Chaya was 6 — their wild giggling and commotion got on the family's nerves, especially during the Friday-night meal.

As soon as the two were done eating, they would retire to the living room and begin their insanity. Their laughing and running around would build up to the point at which the other family members would start shushing them. That only made them wilder. Then the parents would step in, lecturing them about Shabbos and manners. Tempers flared, but in their silly mood, they found that funny too.

One Friday afternoon, the children's mother took each of them by the hand and showed them their own special spots: one in the den and another in the kitchen. "These are silly stations," the mother explained. "It's where people go when they are acting silly. So Eli and Chaya, if you act silly tonight you are each going to be asked to go to your own silly station. You will stay there till Mommy says that it's time to go out."

That night, the twosome behaved as always. But instead of repeatedly shushing them and then becoming angry, their mother said, "O.K., that's enough now. Go to your silly stations." The children looked at each other as if to say, "Is this for real?" But with one glance at their mother, they saw that indeed it was real. They went to their assigned spots and a few minutes later, emerged with sanity restored.

Stations are an effective way to end behaviors that are beneath the threshold for punishment but are still disruptive. Often these situations drag on; the children misbehave, stop when they're scolded and then resume a few minutes later. Unlike time-out, which is explicitly framed as a punishment, stations are presented as a neutral place. Children can even bring a toy to their station if they please.

It is preferable that there be two distinct locations: one for a station and a different one for a time-out. For time-outs, I would recommend a small spot such as a step. For stations, use a couch, area or even a room (one child in the playroom and one in the living room).

Using this technique instills in children the idea that "the table is not the place for silliness" or "the couch is not the place for fighting." Children understand that when they want to eat, they must go to the table. When they want to color, they must do so on paper. When they want to throw a ball, they must do so outdoors. If they are tired, they need to go to bed. Things have their proper place. Stations are the places parents establish for children to go when they have the urge to do something that is not outright wrong, but cannot continue.

Two situations are particularly suited for the "stations" approach. One is, as above, when children get wound up. They are not doing anything bad; they are just overexcited and noisy. They do not need to be punished, but they do need to be stopped, and as long as they are feeding off each other's manic energy, they will be unstoppable. Stations give them a place to regain their composure, and since they know that a repeat performance will only result in them being sent to stations again, they will usually try to stay within acceptable limits when they get back together.

The second situation for which stations work well is low-level fighting. The children are not hurting each other; if they were, a harsher measure would be needed. Instead, they are annoying each other, whining over minuscule provocations such as "She looked at me!" There is no aggressor and no victim, just a constant cycle of back-and-forth needling and complaining. The children haven't done anything worthy of punishment. A parent cannot reasonably expect to control whether or not one child looks at the other. Nevertheless, if the parents are unable to ignore the situation, they can instantly stop the cycle by sending children to "fighting stations." By doing so, the parent is basically saying, "If this is how you're feeling, this is where you need to be while you have that feeling."

Unlike time-out, stations do not involve a pre-set length of time for which the child must stay in his place. Sometimes they work almost instantly by breaking the behavioral cycle and releasing the children from its grip. However, the parent is the one who decides when the child may leave the station.

Despite the neutral tone of this technique, children may experience being sent to their stations as a punishment, and may protest or balk at it. Therefore, parents should have a backup strategy. For instance, children can be told that if they refuse to go to their stations, they will be given a time-out.

It's important to keep in mind that stations, like the other Level 2 tools presented in this chapter, are not long-term solutions. Just because a family has established fighting stations does not mean that the children will stop fighting. That goal may require Level 3 training. However, the stations and other Level 2 tools do give parents a way to end the negative behavior as it is happening. In addition, these tools, when used consistently, tell the children that the family has defined limits of acceptable behavior. They know that if they do X, they will be stopped. Eventually, they may just give up trying to get away with X.

Establishing Family Rules

When we drop a glass on the floor and it breaks, we would never consider arguing with the glass, the floor or the power of gravity. Glass is breakable, floors are hard and gravity will bring the two together at a pre-determined velocity. The result is something ingrained in Creation; it's not a matter for dispute.

Family rules help put parents' expectations of their children on a similar footing. They make certain behaviors a natural part of the family's universe; the consequences of veering from those behaviors are similarly presented as the family's own personal "laws of nature." Establishing rules and teaching them to our children is a firm, consistent approach that will eventually lead them to understand that things work a certain way in our family. Rules also give children autonomy and responsibility for their own fate. Rather than being "bossed around" by their parents, they learn the rules and choose whether to abide by them or bear the consequences of breaking them.

As with all the other Level 2 techniques, a calm, firm approach is key to establishing and enforcing family rules. The trigger can never be "because I got Daddy mad." The child has to perceive consequences as the result of something over which he has control: his adherence to the rule. If consequences only kick in when Daddy is irritable, then the effectiveness of this technique is lost.

A mother who spent much time and effort making child-friendly, nutritious dinners faced a family of picky eaters who ignored their meals and held out for dessert. Concerned that they should at least consume enough calories to keep going and fill their stomachs with something, she allowed them to eat as they preferred.

However, she did not feel good about her approach. She knew she was selling out their long-term health for short-term peace. She needed a way to get them to take a few bites of the food on their plates.

The parents got the family together and announced a new rule: Whoever took a bite from every food on his plate would get dessert. Whoever did not try their food would not get dessert.

The first dinner under the new rule was chaotic. The children protested when they discovered that their uneaten dinners had been removed from the table and their desserts were not forthcoming.

The mother calmly answered, "I'm sorry that you won't be getting dessert. The rule is that those who try their food get dessert. I see that nobody tried their spaghetti and nobody tried their meatballs and only Miriam ate a little bit of her carrots."

The children tried bargaining. "We'll start tomorrow night," said the oldest. "We didn't remember," another child offered in defense. But the mother held firm, pointing to the rule which she had posted on the refrigerator for all to see, which even included a pictograph for the pre-readers.

It was a hard night for the mother. She felt miserable thinking her children were going to bed hungry. They tried to change her mind up until the last of them fell asleep. The next night, however, the entire feeding issue was over. They each tasted each food on their plate.

Rules are an appropriate tool for recurring situations. For instance, a parent who has trouble with a demanding child can make a rule that "If we don't ask nicely, we don't get answered." The child will understand, the second his whining demand is met with silence, that the "ask nicely" rule has kicked in. Other rules parents have found helpful include:

- Clothes that are not in the hamper will not get washed.
- Toys that are left out will be put away for a week.
- If you spill something, you are not allowed to leave the room until it is cleaned up.

- No one leaves the kitchen until the table is completely cleared.
- You have to be at least 10 years old to sit in the front seat of the car.
- Whoever sings *zemiros* at the Shabbos table gets double dessert.

These rules are only suggestions and examples of rules that have worked for others. The best rule for the parent to follow is to use common sense. For rules to be effective, they should be simple to understand and simple to enforce. There should be as little room for negotiation as humanly possible. For example, we included in our list above a rule that toys which are left out will be put away (out of circulation) for a week. Imagine this scene:

Gila takes out her doll, along with the doll's crib, high chair, clothes, blankets and fake baby food. She plays happily for awhile when along comes Rina, her little sister. Rina joins in, but Gila is now finished.

As she starts to put the toys away, Rina says, "Leave it out. I want to play."

Gila obliges and goes outside to jump rope. Rina plays for awhile and then runs off, leaving the toys strewn across the floor.

The mother comes in, sees the mess, tosses the whole thing into a garbage bag and stashes it high on top of the storage closet.

A dispute of Talmudic proportions will no doubt ensue. Gila, who was trying to be generous, is paying the price for Rina's carelessness. She is losing access to her favorite toys. On the other hand, the toys were left out; if the mother wants the rule to stand, she knows she has to be consistent about enforcing it. The point the mother learns from her dilemma is that the best rules are those that leave no gray areas. She amends the rule to say, "Whoever takes out the toys is responsible for putting them away."

On a less formal level, the parenting technique of "logical consequences" follows the same methodology as setting rules. When parents simply allow children to experience the consequences of their unwise behavior, they learn that the behavior in which they have chosen to engage carries with it an inevitable and unpleasant result. For example, a child balks at getting up for school. The parent says, "If you stay in bed later, you won't have time for breakfast," and says nothing more. If the child must rush out to the bus stop having had no breakfast, he learns the "rule" that time doesn't stand still when he presses his snooze button.

For logical consequences to effectively teach children about life, the parents have to stand back and let the consequences happen. The method loses its effectiveness if parents turn the negative outcome into an occasion for a lecture or a scolding. It fails also if the parents try to mitigate the result. For instance, if the mother shows up at school with a toasted, buttered bagel for her starving child, the lesson will be completely lost.

Pre-setting Behaviors

- *Your sister's wedding is tomorrow night and your 4-year-old girl is brimming with excitement. However, you know that if she stays up past 9 o'clock, she will become cranky and clingy. You've hired a babysitter to take charge of her and get her to sleep, but you know she won't want to leave the action.*

- *It's Shabbos shopping time. Although you are usually able to leave your 3-year-old home with her older sister, tonight she is unavailable and your tantrum-prone little girl is coming with you to the super-market.*

- *It's time to visit Bubbi in the nursing home. You want to take along your 7-year-old twin boys to cheer her up, but you're worried that they'll be loud and disruptive.*
- *After a particularly exhausting day, you decide to skip cooking and take your children out for pizza. Everyone has enjoyed the treat, but you know that when they get home, they will be too wound up to go through their bedtime routine willingly.*

In all these scenarios, the parents can conceivably avoid a difficult situation by preparing their children in advance for what will be happening and how they are expected to behave. In this way, they give their children the tools for a successful venture and may be able to avoid the necessity of coming up with on-the-spot ways to curtail inappropriate behavior.

To pre-set behavior, parents discuss the upcoming event/challenge with the children and help them foresee the issues that may arise. They make clear their expectations and deal with the child's protests before the event happens.

Let's take the above three scenarios to illustrate how pre-setting behavior might work.

Scenario 1: Good Night for All

Temima's 4-year-old, Aviva, cannot stop talking about Aunt Dina's wedding. While Temima is excited to dress up her little girl and bring her to this joyful family event, she also wants to make sure that her overtired little girl doesn't prevent her from dancing with her only sister, the bride.

Therefore, Temima hires a babysitter. The plan is that the bride will dance with Aviva for a moment or two, and then the babysitter will take her into the bridal suite and put her to bed on the cushy couch that is there. But how will Temima get Aviva to go with the sitter?

"Aviva, I'm so excited for Aunt Dina's wedding!" Temima tells her one night before bedtime. "It's in just three more days! Let's talk about everything that's going to happen at the wedding, O.K.?"

Temima walks Aviva through the procedures from the kabalas panim to the big entrance of the bride and groom. "After Aunt Dina dances with Bubbi and her chassan's Mommy, she's going to dance with you and me!"

Temima grabs Aviva by the hands and does a practice whirl around the floor, singing "Od Yeshama" for good measure.

"And then, it's going to be bedtime for Aviva. Chavy Goldner is going to take you into the beautiful bride room and get you in pajamas and give you a snack and read you a story and you're going to cuddle up on a soft couch and go to sleep.

"Now listen, Aviva, you might say you're not tired yet, but if you go with Chavy nicely, you'll have a special prize in the morning. Mommy will be right in the next room and in a little while, Daddy and I will scoop you up from the couch and carry you home with us."

Temima lets Aviva choose the snack, bedtime stories, blanket and comfort toy to take with her to the wedding hall. "Let's see how you're going to get all cozy on the couch," Temima prompts. They bring the chosen blanket and toy to the living-room couch and Aviva snuggles into the cushions and theatrically closes her eyes.

Temima rehearses the scenario several times over the coming two days and reminds Aviva about the prize she will get. By the time the event arrives, Aviva is excited about the bedtime plan. She takes her whirl with Aunt Dina and runs into her babysitter's arms, ready to put the plan into action.

Scenario 2: The Supermarket Peace Plan

After many years of parenting, Naomi has a firm rule: no pre-schoolers on shopping trips. Tonight, however, the daughter who usually baby-sits is at her school play. Before Naomi loads 3-year-old Tamar into the car, she has a serious talk with her.

"Tamar, do you want to have fun shopping with Mommy for Shabbos? Can you be a big helper?"

Tamar is delighted.

"You're going to see lots and lots of nosh and yummy food at the store, Tamar. You can pick out two things for Shabbos and one thing to eat while we are shopping. O.K.? After we pick out those things, you might still want to buy more. So then you have to say, 'I already have enough nosh. I'll get more next time.' Let me hear you say that.'"

"I already have enough nosh," Tamar says in her most motherly voice. "I'll get more next time."

"Now let's pretend that you already picked out your Shabbos nosh and you've already got a bag of potato chips to eat while we're shopping. And now, guess what? We see a big bag of red heart lollypops, just the kind you like! What are you going to say?"

"But I want the lollypops!" *Tamar responds.*

"Yes, I know you do. But we can buy more nosh....."

"Next time!" *Tamar responds.*

The mother sets up several other imaginary challenges, until Tamar has her response down cold. When they get to the market and Tamar predictably begins to abandon her strategy in favor of kvetching for a bag of sour sticks, her mother prompts her: "I know you want the sour sticks, Tamar, but we can buy more nosh...."

"Next time!" *the child says, proud that she knows just what to answer.*

The 10 minutes that the mother invests in pre-setting her little girl's behavior pays off in a tantrum-free shopping trip.

Scenario 3: The Bikur Cholim Brigade

Naftali's grandmother is in a nursing home recovering from surgery. She has a special soft spot for Naftali's 7-year-old twin boys, and so of course, he wants to bring them along for a visit. However, they are as rambunctious as boys can be, and he is afraid that they will make so much noise and run around so wildly that they might disturb or even injure the other residents.

"You can do a big mitzvah going to see Bubbi in the nursing home," Naftali tells the boys. *"But you can only come if you remember how to act in a place where there are old people and sick people. They are there to get lots of rest and get better, so we can't make noise. We can't yell. We have to talk in a nice soft voice so we don't wake anyone up who is resting. Let me hear how you're going to talk when we get there."*

"I'm going to talk like this," one twin says in a hushed tone.

"I'm going to talk like this!" says the other in something barely above a whisper.

"O.K., great!" Naftali says. *"And the other thing you have to remember is that you can't run there. You could bump into an old person walking with a cane and chas v'shalom hurt them very badly! You have to walk with me, right next to me in a line, O.K.? Let's try it."*

They march three abreast across the living-room floor. The boys are laughing but they are also getting the idea.

When they arrive at the nursing home, Naftali reviews the plan once more. "Remember two things. Talk softly and walk with me. Are you ready?"

"Ready!" the boys call out.

The visit goes beautifully. Naftali doesn't have to chase them or quiet them down, Bubbi gets a dose of cheer and the family departs before the boys begin to lose their resolve.

Scenario 4: Home Sweet Home

Ahuva's four children are strapped into their car seats, sharing a bag of leftover French fries as they head home from a rare dinner out at Pizza Perfect. It was just the break Ahuva needed after a particularly grueling day, but now she is worried. The children are off schedule and that usually means a long, drawn-out bedtime for which she had neither strength nor patience at the moment.

"O.K., everybody, listen to Mommy. Are you listening?" she calls.

"Yeah!" the four respond together.

"Let's make a plan. When we get home, everyone is going to take off their coats and go straight up to their rooms and put on pajamas. Then as soon as you have your pajamas on, you're going to run to the bathroom quickly and brush your teeth. And if everyone is in pajamas with their teeth brushed by the time the clock says 8:00, then Mommy will tell you one extra story before bed. Is it a deal?"

The children agree. Then Ahuva drills them: "What's the first thing we do when we get home?" They shout, "Take off our coats."

"Then what?" she asks. "Get into pajamas."

"And…" she prompts. "Brush our teeth!"

"And if everyone is ready at 8 o'clock, what do you get?"

"One extra story!" they shout.

They rehearse the scene twice more on the way home. As soon as the car parks in the driveway, the children are ready to spring into action.

Your Level 2

Now you are ready to find out how Level 2 tools can apply to your family, giving you a full selection of effective responses to stop negative behavior in its tracks and establish a calmer household. Using the list of Level 2 situations you identified in Chapter 2, identify which are the ones you can most efficiently address with each of the tools we have discussed in this chapter. Remember that some situations might respond best to the "doing nothing" option. For those that require some action, use the guide below to plan how you can implement the right tools for your family's specific needs.

Level 2, Taking Action

Write down the situations that require taking action, and what action you will take.

Situation	Action I will take

Level 2, 1-2-3 Time-Out

Using the list of Level 2 situations you identified in Chapter 2, find those for which Doing Nothing and Taking Action are not adequate responses. Some of these could be situations in which Taking Action does not end the behavior.

Before you start...

- Make a comprehensive list of time-out locations for your house and for places you frequently visit.
- Make a comprehensive list of backups to time-out to use when the child is not going into time-out, is coming out of time-out or time-out is not available:

  Then....

- Write down situations in which you will use time-out, and how you will respond in the event that your child doesn't comply.

Situation	How I will respond	Possible opposition	I will respond by...

Level 2, Stations

Using the list of Level 2 situations you identified in Chapter 2, find those which you think could be handled by using "stations." Write down your plans for implementing the "stations" approach.

Behavior being addressed	Station locations	If child doesn't comply

Level 2, Establishing Family Rules

Using the list of Level 2 situations you identified in Chapter 2, find those for which you would like to Establish a Family Rule. Write down your new family rules and how they will be enforced.

Rule	What happens if rule is broken?

Level 2, Pre-setting Behavior

Using the list of Level 2 situations you identified in Chapter 2, find those you feel you might be able to prevent by pre-setting behavior. Write down the situations and the strategy you will use.

The challenge	Desired behavior	How to prepare child

Level 3: Building Lifelong Habits

In Level 3, we have two complimentary goals: to eliminate improper behaviors and to develop proper skills and habits.

We will use these tools:

- *Immediate Consequences*
- *Positive Reinforcement*
- *Planning the Habit*
- *Charts*

Habits are our default mode. They are the operating system for most of our daily activities. Even when we are doing something that we would want to do mindfully, for example, praying or doing a mitzvah, when we are unfocused or too tired, distracted or anxious to think clearly, we lapse into our habits.

If we have positive habits, we are in luck; we can do the right thing, the productive thing, without having to force ourselves past our internal obstacles. For instance, if we are in the habit of hanging up our clothes each and every night, or making our beds each and every morning, we will follow through on those actions unless there is some earth-shaking reason not to do so. We will feel unsettled, as if we've left some loose end untied, if we leave these tasks undone.

On the other hand, we might find our best intentions foiled by negative habits. Many people find that even after they have successfully gone on a diet and lost the desired amount of weight, they easily lapse into their former, poor eating habits as soon as their guard is down. Someone who finally gets motivated to sort through a disaster of a closet, organizing everything down to the last hanger, may find that it becomes a mess again just a few short weeks later. His resolution to keep things in order quickly surrenders to their far-stronger habit of tossing stuff inside and slamming the door shut.

If we examine our own inner workings in the realm of habit, we can more easily understand the need to help our children develop positive habits and shed those that are counterproductive. Getting them into the habit of certain desirable behaviors has the short-term benefit of ensuring that these necessary things get done without our constant nagging; and the long-term benefit of equipping our children with a healthy default mode that will serve them well throughout life. Training them away from negative habits, similarly, removes a source of stress from our household and relieves the children of carrying a burdensome behavior into adulthood.

Level 3 is the place for all our parenting interactions that are geared toward these long-term, practical results. There is a great deal of overlap between Level 2 and Level 3, but there is one primary difference: in Level 3, we are focusing on changing the *person*. This means that we invest our efforts in a "training program" of some kind, which by definition may not show its efficacy until days or weeks later. In contrast, Level 2 techniques are focused on changing a *situation* and are designed to work immediately.

For example, parents might have a goal of getting their children to settle down for the night. A Level 2 response, focused on fixing the situation, might be to make a rule, "If you ask for a snack after you go to bed, you have to go to bed 10 minutes earlier the next night." A Level 3 tool, focused on training the child, might be to make a chart that enables the child to earn a prize after five nights of going to bed without calling out for a snack.

Both techniques can be used, even simultaneously, but each accomplishes something different. The Level 2 rule and consequence address the immediate situation. The child has the urge to call out for a snack, but perhaps holds himself back in order to avoid the unwanted consequences. If the consequence disappears, for instance, if he is being watched by his kindhearted grandmother who would not dream of denying him a few rounds of cookies and milk, then the behavior quickly resurfaces.

Using Level 3 techniques, however, the parents help the child internalize the new behavior so that it becomes his preferred and accustomed way of going to bed. His body becomes habituated to settling down and dozing off when he gets into bed and the nagging desire to get up again is eradicated. Even when his grandmother baby-sits, his response to bedtime is the same.

The unifying concept in all Level 3 tools is to encourage repetition of the behaviors we wish to instill in our children. Repetition creates habits all on its own: no explanations, no lectures, no sparkling inspiration required. The more we can get our children to repeat positive behaviors, the stronger these positive habits will become and the more they will become part of the child's nature.

Understanding the difference between Level 2 and Level 3 helps parents arrive at appropriate expectations for molding positive behaviors in their children. When you recognize that your Level 2 method is not designed to solve the problem in the long run, you do not become frantic when you realize that the child has not yet "learned his lesson." You realize that the situation calls for more than a quick fix; some forethought, planning and training may be necessary to get the results you desire. We should note, however, that sometimes the consistent use of Level 2 techniques does the job of Level 3.

Now that we have discussed what Level 3 accomplishes, let's identify some situations that can be best handled by this approach. These would include: morning routines, bedtime routines, hygiene, neatness and orderliness, tone and volume of speech, table behavior, *davening,* homework, helpfulness, thoughtfulness (such as calling or visiting grandparents, writing thank-you notes, etc.) and interpersonal behavior that curtails aggression and promotes social skills.

We also need to decide whether we are trying to eliminate a negative behavior or build a positive one, or, as is most often the case, both. This will help us choose the right tool for the job. Now let's take a closer look at those tools:

Immediate Consequences

The simplest Level 3 tool is Level 2. As we noted above, by consistently curtailing an undesirable behavior, we can instill in the child the knowledge that this particular behavior won't be tolerated and has no place in our home. This is the tool of first resort when trying to extinguish a simple and newly emerging negative habit. It is a vital step, because every time a person repeats a negative habit, he strengthens it in himself. Therefore, we usually can't afford to sit back and wait for the long-term training to kick in; we have to do something now, and at the same time, consider ways of building the positive behavior to replace the negative.

Naomi and Miriam, ages 9 and 10½, are only 18 months apart. They constantly borrow each other's clothes and hair ornaments, and have recently been forgetting to return what they've taken. This results in items being lost in the heaps of clothing in each girl's room, and frequent arguments as well. Their mother wants to teach them to take better care of their belongings and to respect each other's belongings, both long-term goals. However, she knows that every new instance of irresponsible borrowing only makes the habit harder to break. She institutes a rule: Whoever borrows an item must put it away where it belongs or she is not allowed to borrow for two weeks.

With the institution of this rule, the girls are forced to become more aware of the items they borrow from each other. They are also forced to be more organized about where they put the item when they take it off, thus diminishing their mindless dropping of worn clothing in various piles around their rooms. The short-term consequence acts to end a bad habit and promote a long-term, improved habit.

Positive Reinforcement

Once you have identified goals you can achieve through Level 3, you need tools to reinforce the habits you are trying to instill. Everyone loves to be rewarded, whether it is with love, a hug, a prize or a privilege, and therefore, these tools are the most powerful way to inspire cooperation. We may feel that children should do what they are told simply because we are their parents, and we would be right. However, we can work with human nature to make it easier for them to do what they should. Few of us would do our jobs — even if they are wonderful, helpful or even life-saving jobs — if we did not get paid. Even in the realm of parenting, a notoriously underpaid profession, the rewards of love, closeness, emotional support and *nachas* keep us going.

Praise: The Tool of First Resort

One of the keys to using positive reinforcement is to remember it. Parents are very adept at paying attention to their children when the children are creating a disturbance. "Catching them being good" takes a lot more awareness. We tend to take for granted their positive behavior unless it is something above and beyond the norm. Just doing what they are supposed to do rarely brings our children accolades, yet there is no surer way of keeping the good coming.

Praising a child for displaying a habit we want to build is by far the simplest, most straightforward technique. First of all, it's free and always available. Secondly, the praise builds the child's self-esteem, and thirdly, there is no danger of spoiling the child or getting him hooked on material rewards for his positive behavior.

All it takes is awareness. If you see your child doing something you want to encourage, *grab the opportunity to notice and praise him for it.*

For positive reinforcement to be effective, the child has to experience it as positive and interpret it as sincere praise for the specific behavior we are trying to instill. The TEFS formula describes effective praise:

- **T** is for "touch." Giving the child a warm hug, pat or touch amps up the impact of our praise.
- **E** is for "enthusiasm." Even if you feel like an actor, put a note of amazement into your tone. Go one shade brighter than you think the situation really warrants and you'll probably come across to your child perfectly on key. This is especially important if you tend to be an understated person. Children simply do not relate to understatement.
- **F** is for facts. This is a truly essential element of effective praise. State to the child exactly what he did that has won your recognition. For example, your child hears his baby brother crying and gives the baby his pacifier. When you praise him, you break down this act of giving into all its components: "Aaron, you really helped to take care of Yossi! You heard him crying and you stopped playing with your truck right away and found Yossi's pacifier and gave it to him. And now he's quiet and happy, all because you helped him!"

By reciting the facts of the child's action, we let him know exactly what behaviors we are applauding, which in turn reinforces those behaviors. Aaron now knows that perceiving someone's need for help, stopping his activities to offer the help, taking action on someone else's behalf and making someone happy are all praiseworthy activities. The next time he is in the middle of playing and his help is needed, he is likely to be eager to repeat the amazing feat of stopping what he's doing to help.

We can see how this would be far more powerful than simply saying, "Good job, Aaron. You really helped Yossi!" For one thing, if Yossi hadn't calmed down, or hadn't remained calm for long, all the rest of Aaron's efforts would have seemed useless.

But even a concise "good job" is better than "good boy." We certainly do not want our children to believe that their innate goodness depends on their actions in any given moment. If they are only "good" when they do something positive, then they can come to believe that they are "bad" when they get into a fight or fail to fulfill our expectations. They really are *that* sensitive to our words.

- **S** is for "self." When parents praise their children, the reward in the children's eyes is the parents' admiration. They internalize this reward much more effectively when we let them know how their positive behavior made us feel. In the above example, the parent might add, "I was so proud to see you taking care of your little brother. And you know what? Because *you* got Yossi to calm down, I got a chance to finish the work I was doing. That made *me* feel calm too!"

If you have trouble connecting to the impact of a "self" statement on a child, try imagining the impact of a similar statement on you. For instance, your spouse hears you handling a difficult person on the telephone. Your spouse might say, "Wow, you were so calm." And that would be nice. But imagine if your spouse said, "Wow, you were so calm. When I hear the way you handle yourself, it just reminds me of how smart I was to marry you." The praise has now penetrated several layers deeper into your heart.

Tangible Rewards: The Next Level of Reinforcement

When praise is not enough, or is not the appropriate tool for a particular situation, small tangible rewards can often bring big results. Many parents are shocked to discover that for the price of a pack of stickers or popcorn, they can conquer behaviors that have been robbing them of peace, quiet, sleep or sanity for months — maybe even years. When children can't get to sleep at night or get ready for school in the morning, when mealtimes are filled with tension or the house is a constant wreck, parents may stumble through their days in a state of exhaustion and stress, accepting the widely held myth that "This is parenthood. Get used to it."

There are of course no fool-proof methods, and there are certainly children who, because of their own distinct issues, may not respond to behavior modification techniques. However, the vast majority do. The real obstacles most often come from the parents:

- They may not have planned the habit, as we will discuss below, or
- they may have difficulty being consistent, or
- they may have unrealistic expectations of what their child is capable of achieving at his current stage of life. For instance, if parents are trying to train a 3-year-old to get himself up and

dressed each morning without help, in most cases they will be frustrated.

Properly executed, positive reinforcement using small, tangible rewards is remarkably simple and effective. Here are a few examples to illustrate how this method works.

Case # 1: From a Nightmare to a Dream

Rochel shared a bedroom with two younger sisters. She was a very active child who had difficulty settling into bed. Every night, she would disturb her sisters and keep them from falling asleep. No amount of urging or punishing seemed to get her to stay quiet and the whole household was suffering.

Finally, Rochel's mother decided to get serious about changing the behavior. She invested in a bag of popcorn and began her training program. The first session occurred during the day. She had Rochel lie down in her bed with her eyes closed for one minute, thus earning a piece of popcorn. That night, the mother repeated the procedure five times. Each time Rochel stayed quiet with her eyes closed for one minute, she received a piece of popcorn.

The following night, she challenged Rochel to close her eyes and lie quietly for two minutes, earning herself two pieces of popcorn. She repeated the procedure a few more times. The next night, Rochel had to lie quietly for five minutes to receive all five pieces of popcorn.

The next step was for the mother to stand outside the room with the door open; Rochel again stayed quiet for five minutes for five pieces of popcorn. The following night, the mother stood outside the door with it open just a crack. Rochel fell asleep and got her popcorn in the morning. The last night of the training, the mother did not attend to Rochel at all, but got busy with other tasks. Rochel went to bed and got her popcorn in the morning again. At this point, Rochel was trained to lie down, close her eyes and fall asleep.

Case #2: Sweetening the Whine

The Bernstein children all used the same whiny tone to ask their parents for whatever they wanted any given moment. The whining got under the parents' skin and generated a lot of tension. In addition, they felt that the habit was an unhealthy one that would eventually turn their children into unpleasant, demanding individuals. They decided to institute a "say it nicely and calmly" program to get the children to change their tune.

The parents practiced asking for things "nicely and calmly" with the children, modeling the tone they wanted to hear. Throughout the day, whenever the children used the proper tone, they were rewarded with a chocolate chip.

It didn't take long for the children to figure out a way to "game the system" by asking for everything, all the time, in the nicest, calmest tone they could muster. The parents were more than happy to provide their children with opportunities to practice their new skill, albeit for the sole purpose of receiving more chocolate chips. Soon, the whining stopped.

Case #3: Haste Makes Happiness

The three school-aged Levine children slogged through their morning routine, losing track of what they were supposed to be doing and therefore frequently missing the bus. While their mother was urging one child onto the next task, the other two were inevitably stalled out somewhere along the road to readiness.

The Levine parents decided to train their children to get ready for school quickly and efficiently. They planned the habit, breaking down the necessary tasks into a list of 15 small steps:

1) *Sit up and say, "Modeh Ani"; 2) Wash negel vasser; 3) Put on underwear and socks or tights; 4) Put on clothes (girls) and tzitzis and yarmulka (boy); 5) Put on shoes; 6) Check for any last-minute items that should be in your knapsack; 7) Make your bed; 8) Come downstairs with items; 9) Put coat, knapsack and anything else going to school with you together on couch; 10) Come to table for breakfast; 11) Clear your place; 12) Go upstairs to brush teeth; 13) Take your snack and lunch from fridge; 14) Pack snack and lunch into knapsack; 15) Say good-bye and walk to bus stop.*

The mother reviewed the list with the children, a boy aged 5 and two girls, 7 and 9, and gave each child a Winkie candy at the completion of each step. The children sped around as if they were in a relay race, running to receive their reward at the end of each task on the list. Rather than having to follow her children around urging and nudging all morning, or having them miss the bus when they run back home for a forgotten item, she sat in one convenient location with a bag of Winkies, dispensing them gladly into her children's eager hands.

After two weeks, the Winkies were forgotten but the new routine was solid. The mother used lavish praise to keep the children on track, and offered a night out for pizza after every month of no missed buses.

Tools for More Complex Habits

Flipping Negatives

Sometimes a child's negative behavior pattern is very entrenched or complex. Immediate consequences such as those we discussed in Level 2 may not be up to the job of changing it because the child is running along a well-worn track that by now seems to be sweeping him along in the wrong direction with barely any thought on the child's part. You might imagine the child as a massive train hurtling along a pre-set track in a pre-set direction. As long as he is running along that track, your Level 2 consequences will not be effective in stopping him. You might derail him over and over, but he will continue to follow the track he is on, while you become exhausted from your efforts.

Instead, we have to lay new track that leads him in a completely different direction. If he has been heading south, we have to get him on the northbound rail. If he's been heading east, we send him west-bound. In essence this means we seek a positive behavior that is incompatible with the negative behavior. We can then train the child in the new behavior using the habit training tools we have discussed. Here are some examples of positive behaviors that will divert behavior away from negative ones:

Fighting — Playing nicely

Whining — Asking calmly

Lying — Speaking the truth

Chutzpah — Talking to adults respectfully

Ignoring/disobeying — Responding to parents immediately

By "flipping the habit," we can concentrate more of our effort on building momentum in a positive direction. Rather than constantly being occupied with stopping the negative behavior through negative consequences, we create opportunities to reward the child for positive behavior. Gradually, we find that the new behavior takes over and the old one fades away. The same unstoppable and unthinking momentum that carried our runaway train toward mischief and mayhem now carries him in a productive direction.

Breaking Down Complex Behaviors

"Planning the Habit" helps us break down our goal into the smaller steps so that we can focus our children on manageable achievements for which we can measure (and reward) success. For instance, if we decide to work on getting our children to "play nicely" as mentioned above, we could imagine how amorphous that goal would be to them.

A scream emerges from the backyard playground. Mom looks out the kitchen window and sees 8-year-old Shimon sprawled on the ground and 6-year-old Michael wailing and flailing. Mom opens the back door and shouts out, "I told you to play nicely! Now come in the house, both of you!"

The fighting may stop, at least for the moment, but both boys are convinced that they were in fact playing "nicely" when the other one provoked him. Shimon had been "nicely" playing King of the Mountain at the top of the slide. Michael only wanted to "nicely" slide down that slide, but he was blocked by the "King's" occupation of the high ground. Neither boy learned from this interaction with their mother precisely what responses were expected. What would have qualified as "playing nicely" in this situation? One possibility is that the mother can specify that touching anyone else's body is out of bounds and/or that taking turns is a must.

To train children in a new habit, we need to break it down for them. They have to be able to see the goal in terms of doable steps and to understand what it expected of them. We can work on one or two steps of the new habit if that is appropriate, or we can work on the whole thing at once.

For instance, a father wants to teach his son to keep his room neat. He breaks the habit down into the following steps: Make the bed; put used clothing in hamper; keep papers piled neatly in one place; keep the floor clear; put all trash into the basket and empty the basket once a week. Now the word "neat" is not subject to different interpretations between the father and son. The son's success in building this habit can be measured by how well he completes the steps.

If a child would seem to be overwhelmed by a long list of steps, parents can use this planning technique to work with the child in increments. For instance, in the above example, the father could work first to get the son into the habit of making his bed. Once that was achieved, he could work on keeping the floor free of clutter. Then he could work on keeping the surfaces free of clutter, and so forth, until the entire goal has been achieved. In this way, one new behavior becomes second nature before the next one is introduced.

Some goals that benefit from Planning the Habit include:

- Clearing the table: Remove dishes and food. Put dishes in sink. Put food in refrigerator or panty. Wipe down table. Sweep under table.
- Cleaning up a room: Put away clothes in drawers, closet or hamper. Put away toys in toy box. Throw away trash in trash can. Dust the furniture. Vacuum the rug.
- Get ready for bed: Take shower. Put on pajamas. Brush teeth. Say the Shema.
- Play nicely: Share toys. Compromise with other person. Get help from adult to settle disputes. No yelling or hitting.
- Listen to parents: Stop what you are doing right away. Come to where parent is located. Do what you are asked to do right away. If you have to finish something first, ask permission.

"Planning the Habit" is essentially a preparatory step in training our children, but this first step can determine the success of the rest of the techniques we use. When parents tell me that that they tried a training technique but it didn't work, we often discover that the habit wasn't sufficiently broken down in the first place.

To effectively plan a new habit, we have to put ourselves in our children's places and recognize that they may not fully understand the concepts that are second nature to us. We might relate to their position by imagining ourselves moving to a new city; everyone knows the streets, stores, neighborhoods and shuls that everyone else is talking about. As a newcomer, however, we need specific addresses and directions. Someone tells us, "The *bris* is at Rabbi Rosen's shul," but we have no idea where that shul is located. Neither do we know Rabbi Rosen's full name nor the name of his shul so that we might look it up in the local directory. Also, because we don't know the location, we don't know how long it will take us to get there.

The person who told us about the *bris* gave us information based on a pile of inaccurate assumptions about what we know; we would have no way of following through based solely on his words. Likewise, when we tell our children "play nicely" or "clean up," we are assuming that they understand exactly how to get to those destinations. If we really want them to arrive, we have to tell them exactly where we want them to go, and how they can get there.

Practice Sessions: New Responses to Old Triggers

Some complex behaviors, especially unrealistic fears and phobias, can be resolved by helping the child practice new responses to the situations that trigger the problem. Through this method, we give our children tools to use when they are provoked, and confidence to face situations that trouble them.

Case #1: "You're Just a Watermelon"

Binyamin, a diminutive third-grader, had an archenemy at school: the popular, tall and aggressive Eli. Eli called Binyamin "Itzy Bitzy Binny," a name everyone but Binyamin found witty and amusing. When Binyamin's parents found out that Eli's constant teasing was the reason behind their son's reluctance to go to school, they decided to help him immunize himself against the verbal attack.

First, they listened to his woes. They commiserated with his feelings of humiliation and powerlessness and let him have the cry he desperately needed.

Then, through role-playing, they taught him how to neutralize Eli's taunts. The father played the "nickname game" with Binyamin.

The father would call Binyamin a silly name: "You're name is Cantaloupe!"

Binyamin's role was to respond with an equally silly name: "You're Watermelon!"

"Oh, yeah? Well you're Hamburger!"

"So what? Your name is Hotdog with Ketchup on Top!"

The game continued, with plenty of laughter as father and son thought of more and more ridiculous nicknames for each other. After a few days of playing this game, Binyamin used it on Eli. Soon, finding that his wittiness was outdone by his "victim," Eli lost his incentive to keep teasing Binyamin. The provocations stopped and Eli felt great, having acquired the tools to handle his social issue on his own.

Case #2: No Cause for Alarm

After a couple of accidental setoffs, the fire alarm in the Goldman home became an object of fear for 2½-year-old Chaim Goldman. He refused to climb the staircase where the alarm was situated and cried in terror when his parents carried him past it. To end this unreasonable fear that was making life difficult for Chaim and his parents, the parents decided to desensitize Chaim to the object of his fears.

First, they gave the alarm a name: Alarmy. They explained that Alarmy was the family's friend, whose job was to protect everyone from fire. Then they offered him a treat for standing near Alarmy. Once he was willing to stand a few feet away, they offered him a treat to stand right under it. After some coaxing, he mastered that step. Then the parents offered him a treat if he would let his father lift him up to touch Alarmy. Chaim passed this level as well, offering a few tentative pats to his noisy "friend."

Chaim's next challenge was to listen to Alarmy "singing" from outside the house. He stood with his mother outside the front door as the father set off the alarm. Chaim proudly claimed his treat after a minute of listening to the alarm's shrill noise, buffered by the front door. The "final exam" was for Chaim to listen to Alarmy's song while inside the house. Again, he stood with his mother in the living room adjacent to where the alarm was located. The father set off the alarm and Chaim covered his ears, but he didn't cry or act frightened. He earned his treat.

The next day, Chaim's parents knew that their training program had worked. Chaim sat on the bottom step staring up to the ceiling. "Mommy," he called, "Can I play with Alarmy?"

Level 3: The Right Combination

Often, Level 3 techniques work well in tandem with other levels. For instance, a child who grabs toys from other children in his playgroup needs a Level 2 approach that will stop the behavior immediately: usually, a time-out. However, this approach would work best in combination with a training program; for instance, giving the child a chocolate chip every time he shares a toy. This may seem to be unfair: the pesky child gets a chocolate chip and the good child gets nothing. Actually it's no different than any other situation — this is not an ongoing reward — we are merely using this as a bridge to help the child learn a new behavior. Another option is that every time there is sharing, everyone playing gets a chocolate chip.

In addition, several Level 3 techniques can be used together to address a certain behavior. For example, a 7-year-old child is bossy with her playmates and therefore has few friends. The parents use practice sessions to teach the child how to "let others lead." They enact play situations and rehearse with their daughter such skills as asking a friend, "What game to do you want to play?" or saying, "Here, you can have the doll first." In addition, they use a chart to track the little girl's successful efforts at giving in to other children. They praise her abundantly when she exhibits cooperative behavior with her siblings. In addition, they ask her teacher to subtly participate in a way that other students won't notice, but will keep their daughter on track in school. They offer a reward of a special trip when their daughter earns 20 stars on her chart.

Charts

For all but the most self-disciplined people, consistency is a challenge, especially when applied to a new or challenging behavior. Charts are a way to help our children stick to a new behavior even when their motivation begins to lapse. Charts provide ongoing reinforcement as well, as the stars or checks or stickers mount up to the designated point at which a reward is earned.

In learning new habits, repetition is the magic ingredient. To understand the power of repetition, think about the first time you drove a car or played an instrument or learned a dance. Every step in the process required thought and focus. As a new driver seeking to make a left turn, you had to tell yourself, *Turn on the left blinker. Check oncoming traffic in the right lane. Check what's coming in the left lane. Aim for the center of the lane. Turn the steering wheel left. Straighten out....NOW!* After a few months of driving, however, all these steps happen in seconds. Your hands and eyes seem to know what to do without your brain telling them.

A behavioral chart serves to motivate a child to repeat the desired behavior until it, too, becomes second nature. A child who does her homework every night after supper for two months will be able to swing right into action with little or no coaxing by the time those months are over. Her mind will be gearing up for the task as she clears her place from supper. She will have stored her knapsack somewhere where it will be ready and waiting for her. Her friends will know not to call or visit during her homework time. Even hours earlier, in school, she will remember to pack up papers and books she needs for her homework that night. The habit becomes part of the texture of her life, to the great benefit of the child and her parents, as well, who are now spared the strife that homework often causes.

As with all other behavioral techniques, success in using a chart depends on planning the habit and clearly conveying to the child what exactly he must do to earn a check on his chart. In addition, the parents must offer sufficiently motivating incentives and rewards for the children's success. Otherwise, the child may easily forfeit the reward in exchange for not having to perform an undesirable task: "I'd rather give up a package of gum than make my bed 10 times." Here is an example of how one family used a chart to encourage more harmony among their children.

The word people used to describe the Nussbaum children was "intense." They were constantly competing for dominance and favor in the family, and their interactions with one another were often abrasive. The parents were in despair. What they had hoped would be a home filled with happiness and kindness had become the epicenter of sulking and sarcasm. Where had they gone wrong? Why did their children have such awful middos?

They agreed to try using a chart to motivate their children to change their ways. They didn't hold out much hope, however, because they were convinced that the children's behavior came from some deep-rooted cause that couldn't be altered so simply.

They created a simple chart with 100 spaces. They named it the "considerate chart," and instructed their children to tell them any time they did or said something considerate for a sibling. First, of course, they explained to the children what types of behaviors would qualify for a check on the chart. In addition, they offered to take the whole family out for ice cream when there were 100 checks on the chart.

Instantly, the children began doing things for one another and saying nice things to one another, all so that they could quickly accumulate the requisite 100 checks. "Mommy, Yael dropped her pencil and I picked it up for her!" "Daddy, Ari looked sad and I said, 'Don't be sad, Ari!'"

The parents didn't mind at all; the children could have earned all the checks in two days if they wanted, because all the time they were busy being nice, they were repeating the kind of behavior the parents wished dearly to instill in them. At the end of one week, the chart was filled and the atmosphere in the home had completely changed. The ice-cream trip that the children earned was remarkable because the children and parents all actually enjoyed it.

The parents in the above story used a chart for the fairly lofty goal of instilling a higher level of caring and harmony into their children's interactions. They also used Level 4 tools, which deal with instilling values in children, to support their goal. However, their success with the chart points out an important fact: a lot of what we consider "personality flaws" and inborn traits are actually learned behaviors that can be unlearned. Even if these traits have risen like the Loch Ness monster from the gene pool, they can often be modified and channeled into productive directions through Level 3 tools.

More typical uses for charts include: Tooth-brushing; Shabbos jobs or other household chores; *davening* on non-school days; going to bed and/or getting up on time; doing homework; calling grandparents, aunts or other relatives and so forth.

Your Level 3

Now you are prepared to use Level 3 tools to accomplish your goals for your children. Sort through the situations you described in Chapter 2 and choose those that you feel would best be handled by a Level 3 approach. Remember, these may be situations you are already addressing in Level 2; Level 3 tools will increase the benefits by ensuring long-term change. If you identify Level 3 situations for which you see Immediate Action as the best approach, please refer back to "Your Level 2" in the previous chapter for guidelines.

Level 3, Planning the Habit

List your Level 3 goals. *Plan the Habit* you want the child to develop by writing the positive version of the behavior and then by breaking the behavior down into a set of smaller behaviors.

Item	Positive version	Steps

Level 3, Positive Reinforcement

Using your *Planning the Habit* chart, find steps for which you can use *Positive Reinforcement.* Write out the situation and how you will respond. Make sure your praise follows the TEFS (Touch, Enthusiasm, Facts, Self) formula. For the situations in which praise is not applicable, write the words "Practice Sessions."

Situation	How I will respond

Level 3, Charts

Choose the behaviors you listed in *Planning the Habit* for which you want to create a chart. Plan your chart in the space below, defining the precise habit you want to build; how long or how many times the child must exhibit the behavior in order to earn a check (unit); how many checks are needed to earn a reward and what rewards you are offering; and any additional information, such as items you will need to enact your plan or ways to increase the level of challenge and achievement.

Desired Habit	Chart Unit	Reward	Additional Information

After you have planned your chart, you can photocopy the template below or design your own chart to begin your program.

Level 4: Instilling Values

In Level 4 our goal is for the child to internalize important values. We will use these tools:

- *Teaching*
- *Inspiring*

Well-behaved, socially skilled, productive, responsible, helpful: Could we ask for any more from our children? As Jewish parents, we know that the traits we've just listed are only the foundation for the people we want our children to become. We do not aim only to teach them how to be functional adults, but also to teach them why they are here in this world: the higher purposes and values that make life meaningful. Level 4 addresses the realm of values as a goal of its own. It is more about what our children believe and what drives their actions than the actions themselves, and therefore, the tools are very different.

In Level 1, we learned how to do all we can to ensure that our children do not damage themselves or others: basic survival was the goal. At Level 2, we worked on defining limits for our children's behavior: a functional, calm household was the main goal. At Level 3, we worked on training our children: developing positive habits was the goal.

At the first two levels, our tools might be considered more like excavation equipment: their job was to clear away the counterproductive behaviors to make way for the behaviors we want to build. At Level 3, we began laying the foundation: solid, stable habits upon which a good life can be built.

Now we are about to explore Level 4, where we frame the building. To be sure, we cannot think of ourselves as the sole force constructing the person our child will become. Hashem and the child himself — his *bechirah* (free choice), his innate traits and his experiences outside our home — all help to determine the ultimate dimensions. Nevertheless, we can't underestimate our impact either.

What exactly do we mean by "framing the building"? We mean giving shape to the child's identity as a human being and as a Jew. We mean instilling the values that will guide him through life. These include:

- *Emunah* — Belief in Hashem and the Torah.
- *Bitachon* — Trust in Hashem, knowing He loves and helps us.
- Love of the mitzvos — Seeing our way of life as a source of joy.
- Actual performance of the mitzvos: Shabbos, *kashrus, tzedakah, kibbud av v'eim,* Yom Tov mitzvos and so forth, according to a child's age and understanding.

- Personal responsibility — Understanding the impact of our actions and choices, whether for the positive or the negative.

In addition to these values are the more universal values that most parents try to instill in their children, such as a proper relationship to money and materialism, the value of work, respect for our belongings, loyalty to family and friends, helpfulness, trustworthiness and so forth.

If we examine the values we've discussed above, we realize that there may be many Level 2 and Level 3 components to them. For instance, teaching *kibbud av v'eim* as a mitzvah includes the Level 2 goal of stopping disrespectful behavior. Teaching personal responsibility includes the Level 3 goal of getting children to perform the tasks and chores that are theirs to perform. If we can offer one clear message in this chapter, it is this:

We cannot use Level 1, 2 or 3 tools to achieve Level 4 goals.

Our analogy about building a structure illustrates why this is so. The "excavation equipment" of Level 1 and 2 are destructive forces meant to knock down and clear away behaviors that obstruct our children's healthy development. But at Level 4, our goal is to build. Excavation equipment has *never* built anything, and it will not build our children either.

At Level 3, where we are actually doing some construction (of positive habits), the tools are simply inadequate to achieve our Level 4 goals. We can train a child to get to *minyan* on time, and that is an essential foundation. However, it is a far cry from the Level 4 goal of helping a child form a lifelong, meaningful connection to Hashem that will carry him through all of life's ups and downs. "Being there" might be 90 percent of success, but it's the other 10 percent that makes being there worthwhile.

For the above reasons, we have to be very clear in our minds when we are trying to work toward a Level 4 goal. Life does not allow us to neatly divide our parenting interactions: "Sunday we'll concentrate on Level 1; Monday is for Level 2; Tuesday, Level 3; Wednesday, Level 4; Thursday, Level 5 and Friday and Shabbos, we'll just let things fly." On the contrary, everything is going on at all times. Therefore, we have to be able to discern what we are really trying to achieve at any given moment and make every effort not to use our "excavation equipment" to build the masterpiece of a faithful, joyful Jewish man or woman.

There is only one way to achieve this goal, and that is to instill in our children a love and excitement for the values we treasure. Of necessity, they will experience many religious observances as restrictions or obligations. Our job at Level 4 is to put this sometimes difficult work into the context of an exciting journey on a beautiful path.

We can see our role as guides on a challenging but inspiring mountain hike. We keep pointing out the fabulous views and encouraging them to get to the next level, where the view is even more awesome. We hike right alongside them, rallying their strength when an extra push is needed. We make sure they take the right equipment and that they have a chance to rest and recoup when needed.

What we don't do is: yell at them to hurry up, scold them for complaining, send them up ahead while we take a break, complain about the heat and our achy muscles, or worst of all, march them along relentlessly, never drawing their focus to the awesome beauty along the way. When they complain, "I'm tired. It's too hard. I don't want to do this anymore," what we don't say is, "It doesn't matter that you don't like it. This is what Hashem wants you to do and you have to do it."

Level 4, Teaching and Inspiring

Teaching and inspiring: these are the only tools that work. Within those categories are a whole range of options. All of them are meant to create positive associations with the values we wish to instill. In fact, the positive association does not even have to be related to the value we are trying to teach. It can simply be a positive experience that accompanies the child's efforts. We all know the custom of having a 3-year-old lick honey off the letters of the *alef-beis* so that the first association with Torah learning will be that of sweetness. We can replicate this idea in many ways for the many diverse purposes that fall within Level 4.

When the three Greenwald children woke up one Tuesday morning, the oldest peeked out the window and saw a thick layer of snow on the ground. "Snow day!" he exulted to his younger sisters, aged 6 and 3. He ran to find his mother in the kitchen.

"Do we have off?" he asked urgently. "Did you call the snow number?"

"Too early," she replied. "I can call in 10 minutes."

Within those 10 minutes, the boy, Eliezer, had a whole day mapped out. A snowman, a snowball fight with his next-door neighbor, sledding down the hill at the park, cocoa…he couldn't wait. But his bubble was soon burst: "There's school today," his mother informed him. "Starting an hour late." The girls' schools, however, were closed for the day.

"It's not fair," Eliezer complained. "I hate yeshivah. Why do I have to go to school when the girls get to stay home?"

Here, Eliezer's association with Torah learning takes on a negative taste. His fun has been ruined and, insult of insults, his sisters are getting a day off. His parents step in with a Level 4 tool to turn the situation around.

"I know you think it would be fun to stay home," says Eliezer's father. "But you know what? You're going off to learn Torah and you need a good breakfast to do such a special job. Let's go out to Bagel Heaven for breakfast and then I'll drive you to school. What do you say?"

Eliezer cheered up at the thought of a delicious Bagel Heaven cinnamon bun and a hot cup of cocoa. He dressed quickly and father and son enjoyed a warm, sweet hour together before yeshivah began. The father pointed out all the *kollel* men filtering in and out of the shop buying coffee and breakfast on their way to yeshivah. By the time Eliezer got out of the car at school, he was proud to be "one of the men" forging through snowy streets to get to yeshivah.

The positive association was fortified on Shabbos when Eliezer's father read the family a story. It was about a great snowstorm that took place in Europe in the years before the war. The students at a renowned yeshivah, filled with dedication as they were, would not think of taking a "snow day." One by one they bundled up and headed outside, expecting to tramp through piles of snow to get to their destination. To their surprise, however, a path had been shoveled all the way to the door of the *beis medrash*. They later discovered that the Rosh Yeshivah himself had gotten up in the early hours of the morning to shovel the path so that his students would not lose time getting to their learning.

Now Eliezer not only associated going to yeshivah in the snow with a special treat from his father, but also with the heroic devotion of a renowned Torah figure and his students. His father pointed out how Eliezer was "just like them," putting his learning above the convenience and pleasure of the moment. His parents had succeeded in removing the negative association with learning and replacing it with a host of positive associations from cocoa and a cinnamon bun to true spiritual heroism.

By contrast, imagine the scene that would have evolved if they had employed a Level 2 tool instead.

"You have school today, Eliezer, and you have to go. Things aren't always fair. Now go get dressed," the mother states firmly.

"Please, can't I stay home?" he whines. "Shira and Devorah are staying home. Why can't I?"

"Let's get moving. No more arguing. Go, Eliezer, or you're going to be spending part of your extra hour in time-out."

Eliezer would have gone to school. The behavior or arguing and stalling would have been curtailed. However, the incredibly valuable internal growth that occurred in our Level 4 scenario would not have taken place. Instead, a grumbling, resentful little boy would have gone off to school feeling cheated.

Another area in which parents commonly need Level 4 tools is in nurturing a love of Shabbos. For some children, the day feels like an unbearable drag in which their favorite activities are forbidden. The meal can seem long and drawn out and the constant contact with siblings and parents can feel suffocating. As boys come of age to go to shul with their fathers, new areas of contention may arise.

There might be Level 2 or 3 goals involved in getting the family's Shabbos to the level the parents desire. For instance, the children's behavior at the table might be an issue. The parents might use "silly stations" to tame their giddiness, but they must be careful not to address the larger Level 4 issues when sending the children to their silly stations. Parents should concentrate on the behavior alone: "You're so silly right now that you need to go to your silly stations until you can calm down." Those words impart absolutely nothing about the holiness of Shabbos, and they should not, because we do not want to associate Shabbos with anything negative.

At the same time, Level 4 is the essential piece of the picture. We want to foster a love of Shabbos, a sense of eager anticipation for the day. Warmth, love and humor should be the pervasive mood. A child who thinks of Shabbos as the day he gets yelled at, *potched* or humiliated will not grow to love Shabbos. In families where the father is not home much during the week, the relationship between the father and the children can deeply color the relationship between the children and Shabbos. They can either look forward to the extra love and attention, or dread the extra scrutiny and discipline.

Even assuming a normal, balanced relationship between parents and children, all parents need ways to endear Shabbos to their children. There are many simple tools we can use:

- Special candies and treats purchased just for Shabbos;
- Clothing they're excited to wear;
- Toys and games reserved just for Shabbos;
- Shabbos-table stories or games that engage the children;

- Special time with one or both parents. For instance, there might be a good book the parent reads chapter by chapter over the course of several weeks, or a game the parent plays with the child only on Shabbos. This doesn't have to take more than 10 or 15 minutes;
- Special guests or outings; for instance, visiting a nearby relative.

Overall, anything our children particularly enjoy, anything we might allow them in small doses but not only a daily basis, such as candy, or any special attention we can give them, can be reserved for Shabbos, thus adding to their anticipation of the day. We know that candy, outings and games are not the essence of Shabbos, but it does not matter. At this point in their lives, we simply want to teach their hearts to look forward to Shabbos and to bubble with happiness when they see those candles lit. The higher meanings are of course vital, but by creating positive associations, we give them the emotional fuel to seek the higher purposes.

At the same time, we can and should teach them what Shabbos is really about and how precious it is to the Jewish people. We can do this through stories found in books or from real life. We also do this, intentionally or not, through role-modeling. Little we can do or say is as instructive as our own look of contentment as we take that first swallow of Kiddush and that first bite of challah.

Another highly effective way to teach values is to involve our children whenever possible in our *chesed* and other values-driven activities. In doing so, we give them their own "stake in the business" and motivate them to care about its success. We also reduce the likelihood that they will develop a negative association: *chesed* means that Daddy or Mommy has no time for me. Instead of feeling excluded and left behind, they feel involved and important; meanwhile, they are learning firsthand the value of giving to others. Although involving children in our activities is not always possible, wherever it can be done, it provides the perfect teaching moment.

Hadassah was the neighborhood "organizer." She was on the phone day and night arranging whatever needed to be done. When people had simchos, she got everyone baking. When people had babies, were ill or sat shivah, she organized meals. She established a weekly Shabbos shiur for her shul's women and lined up the speakers.

One Sunday, her 9-year-old daughter, Sara, made a request. "Can you take me shopping this afternoon for new shoes? My feet grew!"

"Oh, I'd love to, sweetie, but today's the day I take Mrs. Perlstein shopping and she really counts on my coming."

"It's not fair!" Sara complained. "You're always too busy for us! I wish I were an old lady and then you'd have time to take me shopping too!"

Hadassah realized that a critical parenting moment had arrived.

"I have an idea," she told her daughter. "If you come along, I can finish up with Mrs. Perlstein a little quicker. You can help me load her bags into the car and take them into her house and you can help us put the stuff away. With two of us it will end up taking half the time. Then we can go shopping for shoes. What do you say?"

Sara went along. Mrs. Perlstein was delighted with the company and indeed the job was finished in record time. Hadassah made sure that the ensuing shoe-shopping expedition was especially fun. She gave in on a style that was a little more "grown-up," explaining that Sara had really shown herself to be a little more grown-up.

This situation could have been handled on Level 2 with an immediate consequence for arguing and complaining. However, if the mother had taken that route, she would have reinforced a negative association with *chesed*. "*Chesed* is what takes my mother away from me. *Chesed* means I have to wear tight shoes until my mother has time to take me shopping, which will be *never*."

Instead, Hadassah wisely assessed her real goal in this parenting interaction, and chose to teach a value rather than modify a behavior. She not only avoided reinforcing a negative association, but she also forged a highly positive association. Sara got to see the good her mother actually did; Mrs. Perlstein's frailty and her gratitude for the help were obvious. Sara got to feel that she was part of that good; she had really helped someone in need. All of this was sealed into Sara's consciousness with the happy memory of a shopping trip and her mother's recognition that she was becoming more mature.

For Hadassah, the experience set a new template. She began involving her children in her activities more often. Sara became the official second-in-command for Mrs. Perlstein's shopping trips and as she got older, took on other jobs as well.

How We Project Emunah and Bitachon

"Do as I say, not as I do," is the emblematic motto of poor parenting. No amount of positive teaching can undo negative role-modeling, and therefore, our job of helping our children to grow forces us to grow as well. There are many, many books in Hebrew and English, from classic *mussar sefarim* to collections of contemporary stories, which are aimed at helping each of us energize the lifelong, uphill struggle to hold onto our faith and trust in Hashem when the going gets tough, and to recognize His hand when things are good.

Obviously we cannot touch all these bases within the scope of this book. We only seek to raise your awareness as parents, to reawaken you to the fact that our children learn these values from us on a constant basis. Children possess an exquisitely sensitive radar system that sounds a shrill alarm whenever they detect inconsistency or hypocrisy. They may not be able to articulate what they are feeling, but they feel it. Therefore, we have to strengthen and teach ourselves while we teach them. Here are some of the subtle ways our values come through:

- Dealing with delays: Do we become anxious and lose our temper, or do we accept that things are progressing according to "Hashem's timing"?

- Facing disappointment: Do we dwell on what we believe could have been and should have been, or do we process the setback and say, "Where do we go from here?"

- Money problems: Do we fret or worse yet, fight with our spouse over money, or do we recognize that "We've got food and a home and clothes to wear, and Hashem takes care of us every day"?

- Other people: Are we critical? Exclusionary? Do we foster feuds and hold grudges? Or do we focus on others' good qualities and try to empathize with their challenges?

- Our place in life: Do we envy others for their money or position, or look to ourselves to see how we may be able to improve?

- Risks: Are we excessively fearful and protective, or do we live our lives with a combination of commonsense caution and trust in Hashem's protection?

- Mitzvos: Do we feel that they are an annoyance, an expense and an interruption in our "real lives," or do we take the time to truly embellish and relish them?
- The world: Do we find an appreciation of nature to be a bit "head in the clouds" or do we notice and point out the wonders of Creation?
- *Hashgachah Pratis:* Do we notice and point out Hashem's involvement in our lives and in the world, or do we take it all for granted?

These are just some of the ways our children learn about the values we really hold. Sometimes we actually *do* have a grip on the positive values we want to impart, but simply do not realize how important it is to communicate our beliefs to our children. For instance, we may look up at a night sky and think, "Wow, what a vast universe Hashem created." That is a sincere recognition of Hashem, but imagine the impact of bringing a child outside and saying, "Look up! Can you picture the minute that Hashem created all those millions of stars, all millions and billions of miles away, all just by saying a few words? Look at them all. How many can you count?"

Even in the ordinary course of a day, we can try to articulate what we know in our hearts to be true, in a way that is digestible for our children. "How's the apple? Nice and juicy? Isn't it amazing that Hashem makes a juicy fruit come out of a dry piece of wood?"

Similarly, we may indeed accept a setback in a way that reflects true *bitachon.* But if we just swallow hard and keep our thoughts to ourselves, our children may not get the benefit of our example.

Without lecturing or trying to portray ourselves as the next subject of a Jewish biography, we can still make the point. "I had really hoped I would get this new job, but Hashem has other plans. We'll see what they are!"

We see from all of the above that Level 4 can be an ongoing, in-the-moment approach to life as it unfolds. It might seem that the only way to produce children with positive values is to be a perfect person. However, many Level 4 tools exist outside ourselves, and can be used to plan our approach to specific goals we have with our children. These include:

- Storybooks;
- Songs;
- Words of *Chazal* and other Torah leaders;
- Family rituals surrounding Shabbos and holidays.

As you look through the situations you listed in Chapter 2, you can now discern which are best handled through teaching and inspiring. You can also review your Level 2 and Level 3 goals to find those that have a Level 4 component. In doing so, you may find areas in which Level 4 would be the preferred approach, or you may find areas for which you can use both approaches: one for the short-term behaviors and the other to foster internal growth. As we mentioned earlier, you should be extremely careful not to create negative associations with the values you wish to teach; address *only* the behavior when using Level 2. For example, if you give a time-out for fighting on Shabbos, it's the fighting, not Shabbos, you should be addressing, even though your goal is to improve the Shabbos atmosphere in your home.

Level 4, Teaching and Inspiring

Write down the Level 4 goals you sorted in Chapter 2 and rank them from most important to least important. Then for each item, list books, stories, *Chazals* and rituals that you can use to Teach and Inspire.

Value	Resources

Level 5: Nurturing Emotional Health

In Level 5 our goal is for the child to process emotions, feel loved and be emotionally healthy. We will use these tools:

- *Validating*
- *Spending Quality Time*

One of the great mysteries of the human condition is that we are each a world unto ourselves. Two people standing side by side in the same place at the same time, witnessing the same scene, can have two entirely different scripts playing out in their minds. What frightens one person might thrill another. What fascinates one person might bore another. What reminds one person of warm childhood memories might leave another person cold. Moreover, one person has no way of knowing what that other person is thinking and feeling.

The paradox is that, despite our inherent separateness from one another, our emotional health depends on feeling appreciated, connected and understood. Nowhere is this more vital than in the lives of our children. Because we are the center of their world, they need to know that we understand and accept their perceptions of life, which is to say that we understand and accept *them* as valid, worthy individuals. This is at the heart of unconditional love.

However, unconditional love does not mean that "everything goes." On the contrary, firm and consistently enforced behavioral boundaries are crucial to growing into a healthy and well-adjusted adult. The key to being an empathetic, validating parent is in recognizing the difference between a child's *actions* and his *feelings/thoughts*, even though they usually occur together. For example:

Actions:

*Chani **hits** Moishe.*
*Sara doesn't **greet** her Bubbi when she arrives.*
*Yehudah **tells** his brother, "I hate you."*

Feelings/Thoughts:

*Chani **feels** angry at Moishe.*
*Sara **thinks** Bubbi is a scary lady.*
*Yehudah **feels** and thinks that he hates his brother.*

The key point is that we strictly enforce *behavior* using Level 2 and Level 3 tools *no matter how the children feel about it*. For example, they may feel that they're not tired, and yet it is bedtime, and as their parents, we have the right and the responsibility of making sure they develop healthy sleep habits. Therefore, we should not hesitate to use our behavioral techniques and consequences to enforce bedtime.

What we learn in Level 5 is that while enforcing bedtime for a child who claims not to feel tired, it is not constructive to try to "change the child's mind." Rather, we need to acknowledge and address his feelings. "It must be frustrating to have to stop your game when you still feel like playing, and now it's time to get into pajamas. That's one…" This is in stark contrast to a parent invalidating the child's perceptions by saying something like, "You *are* tired. Look how you're rubbing your eyes and kvetching!"

What this latter reaction tells the child is, "You don't know how to judge what you feel." Such a message can be poison. It can rob a child of his greatest self-defense tool: the ability to trust his instincts to tell him when a situation is dangerous or inappropriate. On a less dramatic level, it erodes his ability to identify what he really wants, likes and needs in life so that he can make satisfying choices. The converse, feeling validated and understood, is *the* essential ingredient to emotional health.

You can easily grasp the importance of this feeling by imagining its opposite: the person who everyone disregards. What more pitiful plight can there be than having no one take you seriously? To have everyone question your judgment? Negate your perceptions? Belittle your feelings? Treat you as if you're crazy?

Even though children have not yet gained the maturity and experience to arrive at mature perceptions, their feelings are every bit as real to them as ours are to us. If we dismiss those perceptions as invalid, we teach them to distrust their own feelings: "I shouldn't feel this way." He doesn't know *how* he should feel, or why he is so flawed and abnormal as to have wrong feelings. As this message continues to penetrate his consciousness, he grows into an adult who doesn't feel secure in presenting himself and his gifts to the world. He is obstructed in his relationships and career, always doubting the value of what he has to offer.

You might think that such dire results can only develop from interactions we would describe as hostile or abusive. However, the process is much more subtle. For example:

- It's suppertime and your child says he's not hungry. You say, "Of course you're hungry. You haven't eaten since lunch!"
- Your toddler grabs a toy from his older brother. The older brother says, "I hate him! He ruins everything." You respond, "You must never hate your brother. You love your brother."
- You ask your daughter to dry the dishes. She says, "I never get any time to chill out!" You respond, "You haven't done anything since you've been home from school. You had plenty of time to 'chill out.'"

In none of these scenarios could the parent be described as abusive or hostile in any way. In fact, he/she is only trying to move the child past a nonsensical or unproductive perspective and into reality. In all cases, the parent is factually correct.

Nevertheless, the message these responses deliver to the child does not address the behavior in question. It addresses the child's ability to perceive and process his own feelings. It says, "Your perception is wrong. It doesn't count." Day by day, little by little, these invalidating responses erode the child's trust in his own sensibilities.

On the other hand, when we listen to our children with full attention and demonstrate that we understand how they feel, we strengthen the cornerstone of their emotional health: their self-esteem. We teach them to trust their perceptions, even if we must help them to process them and perhaps find a productive way to respond.

Rather than saying, "There's no reason to feel that way," and thinking we've solved their problem, our job is to communicate the idea that, "I understand how you feel even if I don't agree and therefore choose to enforce a specific behavior." Then, when the time is right, we can help the child deal with his feelings if necessary.

Many parents fear that by validating their children's feelings, they are supporting negative or wrong perceptions. If a child tells us that he doesn't need to study for a test because he already knows the material, we might fear that validating that feeling amounts to agreeing that it's O.K. to shrug off his schoolwork. In this case, we might choose to invalidate so as not to appear to be strengthening the child's argument.

Sometimes we invalidate a child's feelings because they run contrary to our value system. For example, if a child is angry about some slight, our first impulse might be to explain to them why the slight was not so bad, or the person didn't mean it. While *"gam zu l'tovah"* (This, too, is for the good) and *dan l'kaf z'chus* (Judge others favorably) are vital principles for Jewish parents to impart, they are values that belong in the Level 4 toolbox. Values are never taught in the midst of conflict and high emotion.

The true Torah paradigm for validation of emotions is the experience of mourning for seven days. When we experience a loss, the Torah tells us to tear our clothes, sit on the ground and cry over it for seven days. There will be a time for acceptance of the loss, but first comes the mourning. Those who come to comfort the mourner are most effective when they give him the chance to express his sadness. He cries, and as he does so, his emotions begin to flow again. Crying over a loss feels good. It flushes the pain through our system and makes room for the healing emotions of hope and acceptance. People who do not have the opportunity to sit *shivah* often find healing to be a longer, more difficult process because their pain is still dammed up inside them.

Likewise, we cannot make our children's opposition or negativity go away by invalidating it. Often parents find that once they have validated a child's feelings, the child himself solves the problem. Once children have vented their frustrations and found some empathy for their plight, they can regain their composure enough to see a solution or let go of the issue. Even if they don't, we still have the Level 2 and Level 3 tools to set limits on the child's actions.

Boruch comes home from school angry. He throws down his knapsack and plops himself on the couch with as indignant an expression as a 7-year-old can muster.

"What's wrong, Boruch?" his mother asks.

"I hate that stupid Chaim! He always takes my seat on the bus next to Shimmy, and then I have to sit with David and he's not even my friend! I hate him, hate him, hate him! He thinks he's so big!"

The mother facing this minirant might have several conflicting ideas of what needs to be accomplished. She wants him to realize that he is not allowed to hate another child, nor is he allowed to say, "I hate…" If she's really trying hard on the *chinuch* side of the issue, she might even want to steer him away from *lashon hara* about the much-maligned Chaim. She might want to advise him to make friends with David, who seems to need a seatmate. On a simple level, she might want him to put his knapsack away properly.

Chances are good that if she follows any of these tacks, Boruch will hear, "Your frustration is not legitimate. You shouldn't feel this way." The other lessons will be completely lost. On the other hand, what if the mother empathizes and validates her son's feelings?

"Oh, boy, Boruch, you really feel angry at Chaim."

"Yeah! He thinks he's Shimmy's best friend and he thinks he's so cool."

"It seems like they make you feel left out. That must be so sad for you. I'll bet you wish you could kick Chaim out of that seat!"

"Well, Chaim can have the dumb seat if he wants. It doesn't make him Shimmy's best friend, 'cause that's me. So who cares?"

Boruch hops off the couch and goes to the kitchen for a snack.

In this example, we see that Boruch's mother chooses to deal with his emotions first, rather than any of the behavior issues mentioned above. She validates his emotions, acknowledging without any judgment the fact that he is angry. She doesn't try to lecture him on the evils of hatred or minimize a situation that, in adult eyes, seems petty. Rather, she meets him on his own emotional turf and recognizes the truth of his feelings. This sends a subtle message to Boruch: "I love and accept you even when you have negative emotions. Your emotions aren't bad. They're part of you and you have a right to feel them."

She also empathizes with Boruch's feelings, putting herself in his place and verbalizing his feelings: "They made you feel left out...." By doing this, the mother eliminates Boruch's need to amplify his complaint any further. Once a person has been heard, he does not need to repeat himself or yell his message louder. He can move on, and that's just what Boruch did.

We see in the above scenario all of the benefits of validation and empathy at work. The child was able to process the issue on his own. He was assured that his feelings are valid and trustworthy because his mother understood how he felt. He was assured of her love, even when he expressed anger and negative feelings. This brief interaction turned into a building block of Boruch's self-esteem and his emotional health.

It is important to note, however, that validation and empathy are not tools designed specifically to make issues go away. That is more of a side benefit that accrues when the issues themselves are not particularly deep or complex. A parent may empathize fully with a child's situation and find that the issue persists. Empathy will not solve the problem, but it will keep the child emotionally healthy and the parent-child relationship intact while the problem is being addressed.

The long-term value of this benefit cannot be overstated. It is what keeps the lines of communication open between parents and their children as the children grow into teens and young adults. As children's lives become more complex and their choices become more life-altering, they can use these open lines to come to us with the issues that weigh on their minds. If we want to be relevant to them as they get older, we have to assure them that they are relevant to us now.

How to Validate

The Simple Approach

The simplest form of validation is to repeat back to the child, in our own words, that which the child has told us. People sometimes feel that this is awkward or useless. Why does the child need to hear what he has just said? How does our echo help him process his feelings? Here's how:

You go to visit your brother in Somewheresville, a place you've never before visited. Your GPS suddenly dies. You ride around trying to find your brother's street, but to no avail. You call your brother and tell him you're lost.

"Where are you?" he asks.

"I'm in a parking lot of an Exxon station," you tell him.

"Oh, you're at the Exxon station. So take a left out of there, then your second right, go to the traffic light and make another right. That's my street."

What does the lost brother realize when his brother says, "Oh, you're at the Exxon station"? He realizes that his brother knows the territory. He knows exactly where the lost brother is. Now the lost brother can have confidence that the directions will be accurate. Had his brother instead responded, "What Exxon station? I don't know any Exxon station," the lost brother would have felt alone in his plight.

That, in a nutshell, is the purpose of repeating the child's statement. "I know where you are. I recognize the territory." You may not be giving the child any new information or ideas; after all, you are only saying what he just said. In fact, however, you are giving the child one big, important new piece of information: "I understand where you are."

Using this simple form of validation requires us to listen fully to the child's words so that we truly do hear, and then repeat his statement back to him in our own words. This way, we do not appear to be parroting him. For example:

"What's for dinner, Mommy?"

"Chicken."

"Again? I don't even like supper anymore. It's always chicken!"

"You've had enough of chicken. You'd like something else besides chicken for supper."

"Yeah. Maybe could you make spaghetti and meatballs some time?"

We might look at the above interchange and think that what is needed here is not validation but perhaps some consequence for being demanding. In fact, if that is a behavioral issue, the parent might respond with a Level 2 tool, for instance by completely ignoring the child's statement or by imposing a consequence. These are valid responses for a Level 2 problem.

The most ineffective, potentially damaging response would be to argue, convince, or persuade: "You *like* chicken. You're just being difficult." This invalidates the child's feelings. He is being told that the disappointment he feels about supper isn't real.

The mother in the above example did not feel the need, in this situation, to deal with the substance or tone of the child's complaint. She simply informed him, through her validating response, that she understood how he felt. She gave him a chance for minimourning over his miniloss. Freed of his negative feeling, he picked himself up and addressed the problem with a polite, reasonable request. Even if he had not responded positively, the family rule of, "We only serve one dinner one time and you only get dessert if you eat it," would still apply.

Advanced Validation

The more skilled we become at validation, the more effective a tool it can become. The higher-level skill is to expand upon what the child is telling us, putting ourselves in his place and articulating what we are fairly certain he must be feeling.

In the "GPS" example we used to explain the workings of validation, the corollary would be for the brother to say, "Oh, you're at the Exxon station. There's a Walmart across the street, right? And you can only make a left out of the parking lot." Now the lost brother feels that his brother not only knows where he is, but understands exactly what he is seeing from that vantage point.

In our interaction with children, the skills that build this higher level of trust are those that say, "I not only heard you, but I can see what you see." In real terms, that means expanding upon what the child is telling us. The more we are able to do this, the more accurately we are able to infer and articulate their feelings, the more effective our validation becomes.

"I just finished coloring the page and Atara grabbed it and ripped it! It's not fair!" says 6-year-old Leah. Her 2-year-old sister stands guiltily behind her, clutching the ripped coloring-book page.

"She ruined your hard work and that makes you angry," Leah's mother responds.

"Yeah! I'm so mad at her! She ruins everything!" Leah continues.

"It's so frustrating to feel mad at a little kid. You feel like there's nothing you can do about it!" Mom says.

"She's lucky I'm not Shimmy (their brother). Cause he would have hit her hand and grabbed the page away," Leah adds.

"Sometimes you wish you could hit when she bothers you. It's hard to control yourself when you feel angry," says Mom.

We might interpret the mother's reaction as approval of Leah's anger, but in fact, she is simply putting herself in Leah's place and articulating the feelings she is reasonably certain her daughter is feeling. She knows that Leah had to hold herself back from hitting her sister. Had Leah hit Atara, the mother would have first employed a Level 2 tool to stop the improper behavior.

Here, though, the child held herself back. Her mother did not have to stop a negative behavior; rather, her job was to let her child know that she had a right to her feelings. Those feeling would not cost her love or approval. Those feelings were not wrong or abnormal. They were the normal feelings that sprung up in a normal child's heart in reaction to what happened. In fact, the mother should praise her for not reacting, thereby accomplishing a Level 3 goal.

Because there is some guesswork involved in advanced validation, parents have to keep their finger on the pulse of the conversation and determine if their projections are accurate. If Leah had responded, "Oh, no, Mommy, I didn't want to hit Atara 'cause we're never allowed to hit," then the mother would have to immediate revise her statement: "You know better than to hit your sister, but you still feel angry."

Shortcuts to Advanced Validation

If this skill appears to require too much "thinking on your feet," parents should not despair. There are simple formulas to use that will help you deliver the validation your children need. They will become second nature to you after you use them a few times, and you will use them often when you see how quickly they work to defuse hot tempers, calm hurt feelings and build your children's resilience. Here are some proven techniques:

The Problem-Wish Technique

When your child voices a problem, there is always a wish behind it. The child has a problem: "I'm so boooooored." The parent verbalizes the wish behind it: "You really wish there was something exciting to do."

Here are some other examples:

Problem: "I'm *boiling* hot! I don't need a coat."
Wish: "You just wish that I would let you go outside without your big, heavy coat."

Problem: "No one likes me in school."
Wish: "You wish you had lots of friends."

Problem: "I hate going shopping! We're gonna have to go to a million places. It takes so long."
Wish: "You wish you could just stay home and play outside with your friends."

This process can also work in reverse. A parent can deduce from the child's wish what his problem is. For instance, in the above example, the child might say, "I wish I could stay home." The mother can validate that feeling by saying, "Shopping does take a long time and it must be pretty boring for you."

What do we accomplish in this Problem-Wish validation? We give the child assurance that we not only hear his complaint, but we understand its meaning to him. Non-validating responses to the above scenarios might sound like this:

Child: "I'm boiling hot. I don't need a coat."
Parent: "It's only 40 degrees. You'll be freezing and catch a cold."
What's missing: Our acknowledgment that the child feels hot and finds the coat cumbersome. Even if it's cold from an objective point of view, the child is still entitled to his own feelings.

Child: "No one likes me in school."
Parent: "Of course people like you. What about Avi and Shmully? They're your friends."
What's missing: Recognition of the child's feeling that he's not as popular as he would like to be.

Child: "I hate shopping! We're gonna go to a million places. It takes so long!"
Parent: "It only takes an hour. We'll be home before lunchtime."
What's missing: Acknowledgment that the child does not enjoy being dragged from store to store.

The Feeling-Situation Technique

Certain feelings arise from certain situations. With a little understanding and forethought, we can articulate that slightly deeper level for our children, assuring them that what they are feeling makes perfect sense, given the situation. For instance, a child says, "I'm angry." The situation that arouses anger is injustice, and so a parent can validate by saying, "Yeah, what happened wasn't fair."

This works in reverse as well. If a child complains, "That wasn't fair," the parent can validate by saying, "And it makes you angry." In both instances, the child's immediate reaction will be, "My mother/father really gets me." Here are some common Feeling-Situation pairs you can tap into when your children express negative emotions:

- Sadness — Loss: People feel sad because they have lost something. It could be an item, an opportunity, a friendship, status or anything else the person values. Therefore, if a child says, "Rena isn't my friend anymore," the parent can validate by saying, "That makes you sad." If a straight-A student gets depressed over a B on her report card, rather than responding with, "What's wrong with a B?" the parent can validate her feeling by identifying her sense of loss: "You're sad to lose your place as a straight-A student."
- Frustration — Repeated Failure: We want to instill in our children the value of persistence and resilience, but first, we need to validate their frustration when success eludes them. For example, a boy is trying to learn how to ride a bike and he keeps falling off. He might say, "I hate this! I'll never be able to do it!" Validating his feelings comes hard to us: We want him to have faith and keep trying. However, we need to acknowledge how *he* is feeling about it. "Wow, it must be so frustrating for you to keep falling off the bike!"
- Bored — Nothing Meaningful to Do: The normal reaction of parents confronted with complaints of boredom are to either suggest a list of activities, all of which are bound to be rejected, or to threaten to "find them something to do" like mow the lawn or clean out the closet. Usually, a child complaining of boredom is not really out of all options. There's something else bugging

him. A validating response to "I'm bored" might be, "There's nothing you really feel excited about doing right now."

Expectations

Usually, anger is the result of thwarted expectations. For example, when a mother is home alone and she has a pile of dishes to dry, she might feel unenthusiastic about the chore, but she isn't angry. However, if someone else was supposed to dry those dishes, she will be angry. She is not angry that she must dry dishes. She is angry that someone who "should" have helped did not do so.

With this in mind, we can often validate our children's feelings of anger by identifying their defeated expectation: "My teacher is so mean! She punished the whole class just because two girls were talking!" says the child. The mother validates, "You would expect that when you're behaving nicely, you won't get punished."

Continuing the Paragraph

This is an expanded form of simple validation, in which we embellish the story they are telling us and fill in the details of the picture. For instance, a boy comes home from school and complains that he was not chosen for a hockey team at recess. He's furious at his friends for not including him. "You felt really left out," the father says, "Everyone was out on the playground having a good time and you were stuck looking for something else to do. You wish your friends would have cared enough to include you."

We might read the above words and feel that the father is foolishly providing the salt for the child to rub into his own wounds. However, the truth is that he is helping the child drain the wound. The father's words will not bring a smile to the child's face; they will, however, give the child emotional space to feel his pain, vent his pain and then get past it. Telling him, "I'm sure they didn't mean to hurt your feelings, and besides, you don't really like hockey," would do the opposite.

Summarizing

After allowing a child to express his feelings, we can let him know that his message has come across to us by summarizing what he has said. Hearing that we've caught every word lets him know that we consider his feelings important. We have focused on his story and we are thinking about it.

For example, in the scenario above in which the child was left out of a playground game, the parent can listen carefully, using simple validation throughout. Then, at the end, he can say something like: "So you were standing out on the playground looking forward to being part of the hockey game, and everyone was choosing up sides and you got left out. Not only that, but it was your own friends who left you out. Then you had nothing to do and you walked around the whole rest of recess feeling very sad and angry. And you're still angry about it!"

Hyper-Wishing

This is an extension of the Problem-Wish technique that injects a bit of playfulness into the equation. Here, the parent goes over the top with the wish scenario, throwing in every dream the child might harbor in that particular area. For example, a child doesn't want to take a bath. The parent can say, "You wish you never had to take a bath. Maybe there could be a magic bath that gets you shiny clean while you sleep. It washes your hair and brushes your teeth, too! And when you wake up in the morning, you smell all soapy and clean, your hair is brushed and your clothes are already on! Maybe we could sell it to all the other kids who don't like baths and we'll become millionaires! What should we call our magic bath?"

Somewhere in the middle of this imaginary scene, the child is laughing at the absurdity of it. However, he also enjoys his parent's enthusiastic willingness to grasp his cause — albeit a lost cause — and take it to the outer limits.

Setting the Emotional Climate

No matter how skilled we are at our verbal validation responses, they will not be effective if the child does not feel that they are coming from a sincere place of love and acceptance. Everyone has suffered through the nonchalant, insincere, "I hear you," which essentially means, "O.K., you had your say. Now go away."

Validation thrives in a warm climate. Time together creates that warmth. In our busy, distracted generation, this essential is gravely endangered, heading rapidly toward extinction. If we did not have the weekly hiatus of Shabbos, we might never have any period of bonding time that isn't interrupted by a ring-tone, buzz or bleep that pulls our attention instantly away from our children. Even when we don't answer the electronic summons, we look to see who we are not answering. These interruptions may take a nanosecond, but they break the continuity of our interaction.

Against this backdrop, finding time to spend one-on-one with our children has become more essential than ever. This is time dedicated to allowing each child to really talk, to express whatever is on his mind, whether it seems trivial or important, valid or misguided, whether the information is welcome or disappointing.

We have to be prepared to hear whatever they have to say and do nothing more than accept it as their truth.

This is not the time for correction. Levels 1, 2 and 3 are there to help us correct behaviors. Level 4 gives us tools for instilling the values we cherish. While we can and do flow from level to level in our everyday parenting interactions, our success depends on keeping them separate in our minds, knowing what we are trying to accomplish in a given situation and using the correct tools to accomplish it.

When we set aside time for bonding and communicating — the interactions that are most precious in building our long-term relationship with our children — we are foolishly wasting that time if we use it to push for lesser gains such as getting our child to brush his teeth. We are like someone who trades a bar of gold for a bag of groceries. We've traded away our most valuable asset. If we use this time correctly, our children will feel safe opening up to us. They will feel understood and accepted, and will want to keep us in their lives as they grow older.

Besides the focused time we spend with individual children, we need to keep pumping warmth into the climate of our homes. We have to find ways to show love to our children, to ensure that they feel valued. This means interacting with our children as people, enjoying their company as we would a friend. So often, we are too busy to engage our children on this basis and our only interactions are directive. We forget to share a joke or a laugh, to turn on some music and sing or dance, to invite them into our world where appropriate, telling them a little about our day or our work.

One mother, whose relationship with her 9-year-old daughter had become confrontational, began asking the child her opinions on small household matters. "We're going to paint the living room. What do you think would look better, beige or peach?" The mother made a point of striking up friendly, non-issue conversations with her child and noticed an immediate defusing of the child's volatility.

Physical affection also goes far in establishing a deep, inner certainty of a parent's love. A brief hug, a kiss, a rub on the back, an arm around the shoulder, holding hands, sitting on the parent's lap are all actions that, at various stages in the child's life, can cement a loving bond.

To convey our love to our children, we have to understand what says love to each of them. It isn't difficult to know; we simply have to become aware of the things they most often ask of us. For instance, one child always shouts, "Watch! Daddy, watch me do a flip!" "Listen to me sing this song!" "Watch me go down the slide!" Clearly, having the parents' attention and admiration is what spells love to this child. Another child may always want to sit on the parent's lap and be read a story. Another wants to go along on errands. Another begs the parents to take part in a board game.

Often, these requests come at inconvenient times. However, if we realize that through them, our children are telling us, "This is how I know you love me," we might find the ability to prioritize differently and give each of them more of what they need.

In a climate of love, with the tools of validation, we have the opportunity to give our children the most "vital organ" of a happy, productive adult life: a healthy heart. Raising children who can give and receive love, rise up from failure and keep trying, trust their feelings and trust other people is to "win the gold" in parenting.

Level 5, Validating

Using the list of Level 5 items you sorted in Chapter 2, write down the situations for which your child needs to process an emotion or experience, and describe how you will *Validate*.

Emotion or Situation	Responses

Level 5, Spending Quality Time

Write a list of **Quality Times** that you will put aside to spend alone with each of your children on a weekly basis to talk to them about their lives and listen to them fully. It can be as short as a five-minute walk or as long as a day out together.

Part 3:
Wrapping It Up

Anger, the Antithesis

Our toolbox is now full. We have identified five different parenting goals and the tools that accomplish each one. Notably, anger was not among them. That is because anger is not a tool, but rather, it is a corrosive force; it can destroy any one of the tools you may want to use, rendering it as weak and useless as a rusty hammer. And like rust on a hammer, anger is likely to cause you to break loose, fly off the handle and miss your mark.

Many parents labor under the illusion that, rather than being a non-tool, anger is their only effective tool. "My kids only listen when I get good and angry," parents often say. In terms of getting immediate obedience, they may be correct in their perceptions. However, their short-term gain will turn into a long-term loss and eventually, even the short-term gains will cease. Here is why:

What's Wrong With Anger?

Anger damages our parenting ability in four critical ways:

First of all, it overwhelms our good sense. We all know the Torah's adage that a person loses his wisdom when he loses his temper, and that proves itself true time and time again.

"Quiet, Shloimie! All this racket is going to wake up the baby!" the mother says sharply.

Nevertheless, 5-year-old Shloimie keeps singing at the top of his lungs. The mother thinks only about the potential disaster if the baby, who is difficult to put sleep, is rudely awakened right now. She'll be in a cranky mood and demand to be held and rocked for the next two hours. Nothing will get done until 10 o'clock at night and the mother is already beyond exhaustion.

"Shloimie! Stop that shrieking right now! Stop it!" she yells louder.

The mother is trying to wash the dinner dishes. Her heart is beginning to race as she waits to hear the unwelcome sound of the baby crying. Shloimie's continued singing, now accompanied by his younger brother, makes her blood boil.

The mother can't take another second of this. She goes running into the living room where the children are playing and screams, "You bad, bad boy! What's wrong with you? Don't you know that Chavi is sleeping? Who's going to take care of her when you wake her up? You? Get up to your room right now and go to bed!"

She gives him a slap and sends him running. The commotion of her yelling and Shimmy crying wakes up the baby.

In her anger, the mother forgets that her own yelling is just as likely as her son's singing to wake up the baby. She continually ups the volume of her reprimand as she shouts from the other room, and then swats Shloimie for good measure, ensuring that he will dissolve into loud bawling. She sends him upstairs to his bedroom, failing to realize that he and his noise will come even closer to the baby. This is not a poor plan; it is no plan at all. It is emotion running wild, defying all logic.

The second problem with anger is the *middos* and behavior it models for our children. The mother in the above scenario engaged in the ironic act of yelling at her child not to yell. Similarly, in our anger, we often use words and deeds that contradict what we want to teach our children. When we thunder, threaten and hit, we show our children that power and authority give a person license to bully others into submission. If we get them to behave by scaring them, we cannot be surprised if they try to get others to do their bidding through the same method. If we use rough, insulting language in our scolding, we cannot be surprised to hear such language emerging from their mouths.

If we lose self-control, we cannot become righteously indignant over our children's loss of self-control. The fact that our breaking point comes after much more stress, or that much more important issues cause us to break, does nothing to mitigate the lesson we are inadvertently teaching.

We might think, *Sure, I snap after I've tried for 15 minutes to get this child to sit down and do his homework. Homework is important. And he has to listen to me. So I have good reason to snap. But he's just throwing a tantrum because he can't have chocolate after he's brushed his teeth for bed. That's ridiculous and he knows it.*

What the parent doesn't realize is that he, too, is "just throwing a tantrum" and the child cannot make a distinction. The child's frustration over the longed-for chocolate bar tests his patience just as much as the parent's frustration over the child's balkiness at homework time. There is no point at which a parent can legitimately say, "I've held it in for long enough. Now I'm going to let him have it." That is, unless he's aiming to teach his child that this is a legitimate reaction to frustrated expectations.

The third drawback to anger is the volatile atmosphere it creates in the home. Imagine living on an active earthquake fault line. You could never relax. You would never feel safe. You would feel that at any moment, disaster could strike. Instead of focusing your energy on proactive, productive living, you would be busy creating and fortifying your defenses.

That is how a child experiences life in a home where angry outbursts are the norm. His world lacks a feeling of safety and predictability. He never knows when the next explosion will come along. Therefore, instead of expending his efforts on growth and achievement, he focuses his energies on staying off the radar, out of harm's way. Fear begins to replace hope and optimism as the lens through which he views the world.

Sadly, so many of us grow up this way that a great majority of people — perhaps many of the readers of this book — find our path to happiness obstructed by these fears. We carry around an expectation of negative reactions and consequences that makes us afraid to try anything challenging, whether it is as simple as introducing ourselves to a new neighbor or as complicated as launching a new career.

What we are experiencing often has its roots in the insecurity of a volatile childhood home. That is where we discovered that "you never know what's going to happen" and that "you better not make waves."

In the opening scenario, the little boy, Shloimie, who was singing at a decibel level certain to awaken his sister, did not respond to the mother's requests to quiet down. The mother employed no actual tools to get him to change his behavior, but rather just kept yelling her directions from her post in the kitchen. The next thing Shloime knew, his mother blew into the living room like a hurricane, called him bad, swatted him and sent him to bed. None of this was predictable by a rambunctious 5-year-old. He learned through this experience that in his world, you can be having fun signing a song and the next thing you know, you've been hit and screamed at and sent to bed. What a world!

To thrive, children need stability. That means predictability. "If I do X, the result will be Y." It may surprise some readers to know that angry households are not necessarily strict households. Sometimes they are just the opposite: uncontrolled, disorganized, *laissez-faire* households in which there are no predictable consequences to a child's actions. The children may get away with a lot more than children in a stricter household; however, when the parents have "finally had it," they explode. On the other hand, the parents who run their home according to predictable expectations and consequences have no need to explode. They have other tools to use, and in using them, they keep difficult situations from careening out of control.

The fourth negative aspect of anger is the danger inherent in fury. If we could dissect the emotion of anger, we would find within it the urge to crush and obliterate the subject of our anger.

Intellectually, that may be far from what we really want, but the emotion of anger has a will of its own. That is why, when anger overtakes us, it leads us to do and say things we regret. No one wants to crush and obliterate his child. Yet an angry parent might deliver a hard smack that physically injures a child, or a scorching insult that crushes the child's spirit. These experiences do not fade over time. The fear and shame of these interactions can last a lifetime, and often do.

Returning again to Shloimie in the opening scenario, let's imagine what motivates his mother as she storms into the living room, screams at and hits her son. She is thinking one thing and one thing only: *The noise won't stop! I have to make it stop! I can't take it if the baby wakes up!* She may not think of this as "crushing and obliterating" her child when she mulls the situation over later, in some quieter part of the evening. But in effect, that's what it is; she just wants to "get rid" of the noise and avoid the trouble it may bring. Since her son is the source of that noise, she just wants to "get rid" of him. That's the inner script of her angry outburst, even though it is by no means her real desire.

Tools for Overcoming Anger

Some of our propensity for anger is inborn. Even as babies, some people are patient and persistent while others are easily frustrated. As children, some will concentrate for hours on a puzzle or a project while others will throw down the pieces and storm away claiming, "This is such a dumb puzzle!" Among teens, some will comply with their parents' wishes and their school's rules, even when they don't like them. Others can't stand a moment of what feels like unbearable limitations. Among adults, some people take offense or lose patience easily and some are forbearing under any circumstances.

Because anger stems at least partly from our personalities, there are some people who have little trouble bringing it under control. They do not possess a particularly volatile nature; they react in anger simply because they have not given much thought to the matter. Yelling and hitting seem to them to be a natural part of parenting and they haven't seen the need to learn alternatives. Once they come to a realization that anger is harmful, and develop better ways of dealing with their parenting challenges, they can lay anger aside without too much trouble.

For many people—perhaps most—anger is a greater challenge. Loosening its grip on our emotional life requires motivation, effort and tools. However, success in this area is not an "all or nothing" proposition. Even if a parent reduces his angry responses by 70 or 40 or even 10 percent, the improvement can have a lasting and significant impact on the household and children.

Many people, when reading this section, might be skeptical. You might be one of them. You might believe, "My parents hit me and yelled at me and it didn't do me one bit of harm. In fact, it did me good." And you might even be correct. But think about it. Even if it did work for you, is there any guarantee that it won't have the opposite effect on your children? With the epidemic of emotional and spiritual difficulties besetting recent generations, does it make sense to use a potentially toxic "medicine" when you can use those that do just as much or more good, without the risk? Remember, eschewing anger does not mean endorsing an "anything goes" philosophy. On the contrary, consistent boundaries and consequences help *reduce* anger.

As a therapist who has had the task of trying to undo the damage of angry parenting — both for children growing up now and for children long ago grown — I am using this page to plead with you, the parents entrusted with raising this generation, to grasp the tools we are about to learn and use them to reduce the level of anger in your home. You can raise good, responsible, obedient and loving children — no matter how many and how lively they are, no matter how tired and spread thin you are — without anger. Here's how.

Tool #1: An Anger Log

Make an accounting of what gets you angry, when and why. Using a small notebook or a digital device, record every episode in which you lose your cool with your children. Include this information:

- Time and date
- Level of reaction on a scale of 1 (mildest) to 10 (strongest)
- The event that triggered your anger (For example, your son missed his bus)
- The expectation or boundary you had in mind that was violated (I expect him to be on the bus so I can get to work on time.)
- What results you achieved through your anger (Maybe he'll be scared to be late tomorrow.)

Tool #2: "Parent Yourself" with Behavioral Tools

Many of the same tools we have learned for altering and channeling our children's behavior will work just as effectively on us.

- Use Level 2 tools to create a consequence for your anger. For instance, decide in advance that you will put money aside for *tzedakah* whenever you react above a certain level on the 1-10 scale.
- Use Level 3 tools to train yourself to react in a different way. Using your log, determine what situations tend to trigger your anger. Develop and rehearse calm ways to handle those situations. Reward yourself when you succeed in overcoming a challenging situation.
- Use Level 4 tools to find inspiration for self-improvement. There are hundreds of books, *sefarim, shiurim,* video and audio materials that deal with the many emotional and spiritual facets of anger.
- Declare your own time-out. When you feel overwhelmed, announce to your family, "I'm angry right now and I'm going to take a break." Then go to a private place for a few minutes and calm down. Your announcement enables you to express the fact that you are angry, thus relieving the pent-up tension somewhat and helping you to calm down more readily. This technique also models excellent behavior for your children.

Tool #3: Diagnosis and Repair

Use your log to analyze what specific factors in your life spark your anger. Once you understand the workings of your anger, you can come up with practical ways to make repairs. You'll be surprised to see how effectively this practical approach changes your reactions.

- Look at your log to understand what your anger does for you. Does it get your children into bed? Does it get them to stop fighting? Does it motivate them to apologize? Now create Level 2 and Level 3 strategies to accomplish those same goals.

- Notice what unfulfilled expectations trigger your anger. Plan ahead to convey those expectations to your children *before* the next episode. For example, if you expected your children to help you clean up after Shabbos but they balked and that triggered your anger, tell them directly and firmly *before* Shabbos ends that "everyone has a Shabbos cleanup job" and let them know what each of them will be expected to do. Enforce your new rule with Level 2 consequences. If you let them stay up late for a special trip and then had trouble getting them to bed, tell them prior to the next such occasion, "If we let you stay up late to go out for ice cream, everyone has to get right into pajamas the second we get home." Your anger is a signal to you that you expect your children to "know on their own" what you want from them, while the reality is that they do not. You will find that when you let them know and you enforce the boundary, that particular trigger disappears.

- Notice what boundaries are being crossed and address the situation, either with new family rules or other tools. For example, you may tend to lash out when your children repeatedly interrupt you while you are speaking to others. Your resentment builds as you think to yourself, *I can't think straight when these kids are around!* Create a rule that lets your children know when interruptions are allowed and when they are not. Include a consequence for breaking the rule.

You may also find ways to avoid an anger-producing situation altogether. For instance, if your young children are cranky and disruptive during the summer's late Friday-night meals, you might give them their own, earlier meal and put them to bed before the adult meal.

Tool #4: Emotional Self-Support

Our children need validation and empathy — and so do we! Fortunately, we can often supply it to ourselves.

Assertiveness: Much of the tension parents feel comes from living the life of the "exploding doormat." We try to be everything to everyone, providing non-stop service to our spouses, children, other relatives, employers and community. Rather than asserting ourselves with a firm, calm "no" when something is beyond our inner resources or violates our personal boundaries, we stretch ourselves past the limit. Meanwhile, exhaustion and resentment are building up inside us. Then we explode.

The victims of the explosion are usually our children. They may be the cause as well; they may be the ones demanding too much from us. Instead of "being the bad guy" and consistently using Level 2 and Level 3 tools to teach them proper limits, we try to "be nice" and "give in" time and time again. Then we snap. Sometimes, however, the children are just innocent bystanders. The parent is already at the bursting point from other people's demands, and the children add that one final ounce of pressure that causes the parent to explode.

The obvious solution is to learn healthy assertiveness. This means being able to say "no" *without explaining or defending yourself.* If this idea seems unnatural to you, you may need a book, a coach or a therapist to help you define your boundaries and learn how to defend them. Remember that you are being far kinder by saying "no" firmly and calmly than by saying "yes" until you explode with destructive anger and aggression.

Validation: Take some private time to talk to "the angry part of you." Listen to what it is telling you and validate those perspectives. Just as we learned in Level 5, listen without judging, without fixing or re-adjusting. Accept that this is reality as your heart feels it, even if your mind "knows better."

Often, in doing this, we learn that a part of us is like a small child who feels terribly unsafe in the world. We feel that our only protection is to lash out; our only way to be heard is to roar. Genuine authority expresses itself with quiet assurance, and therefore, we can be reasonably sure that a lot of thunder and bluster express the opposite.

Patience: For many people, taming and eradicating anger is an ongoing, lifelong mission. As with any effort to change a personality trait, there are setbacks along the way. You may need to try various tools until you find the ones that work best for you. If you are not seeing progress on your own, do not hesitate to get professional help, because the longer you let anger run your home, the more likely you will be to bequeath this destructive trait to the next generation.

Perhaps the most vital tool in this vital mission is the anger log that you keep. From your entries in your log, you will be able to evaluate your progress and determine what still needs to be done. You will be able to zero in on the specific situations that provoke anger in your own life, analyze the components of that anger and work out solutions. Sometimes what seems overwhelming turns out to be entirely doable. You may just surprise yourself.

"I had six kids, all two years apart. The youngest was about 6 months old," recalls Shulamit. *"I never got through a Friday afternoon without blowing up countless times. No one heard me when I asked them to come do their jobs. They fought all afternoon. They made messes where I had just cleaned up. I was so exhausted that I used to fall asleep after candlelighting, leaving my kids to take care of themselves.*

"Then one Friday morning, I woke up with a bad case of laryngitis. I could barely speak, let alone yell. It was the most peaceful Erev Shabbos of my life. Somehow, the fact that I couldn't yell made me calm inside. I got everything done and the kids were more cooperative than usual. I had always thought that if I didn't yell at the kids, we'd never be ready for Shabbos on time. I found out that calmness was not only possible, but it was much more effective. The laryngitis turned out to be a really great gift."

A peaceful home is indeed a great gift. The very word "home" speaks of the place where we feel safe and welcome. It's the place where we can be ourselves, where we are accepted and loved from the moment we walk through the door. By eliminating anger, we create an atmosphere in which our children are not forced to hold their breath in anticipation of the next explosion, but rather, they can relax, exhale, drop their defenses and accept the love that surrounds them. This is what it really means to give a child a home.

The Inflexible Child

*L*et's go, Yaakov! We're leaving for Zeida's house in five minutes and you haven't even got your shoes on!"

"I'm almost at the end of the book," 8-year-old Yaakov tells his father. "I have to finish it. I'll go nuts if I have to leave it right before Detective Duvvy solves the case."

"You can read it in the car," answers Zev, Yaakov's father.

"That makes me carsick," Yaakov replies. "And besides, it's a library book and you don't let me take library books out of the house."

"So read it when we come home," Yaakov tries again.

"But then it's already gonna be after bedtime," comes the ready rebuttal. "Why can't we just leave for Zeida's house a little later? I only have 10 more pages."

"Everyone's ready. All the kids are standing in the living room in their winter coats. Let's move!" Zev answers, anger seeping into his voice. Why, oh why, was everything a problem for this child? Why did he always have to argue?

Yaakov's face turns red as he closes the book. He looks as if he's been cornered. He slams the book on the floor and screams, running up the stairs, "I'm not going! I hate Zeida's house!"

If this scene seems vaguely familiar to you — perhaps the same theme with a different plot and characters — then you may have a child who tends to be inflexible and explosive. Dealing with such a child calls upon your best parenting skills and most refined personality traits so that you can forge a positive relationship and instill self-esteem in the child, even in the midst of conflict. You don't have to be an angel, but you do have to understand what makes this child tick so that you can use your Five-Level Parenting tools to work with, rather than against, his personality.

Understanding Your Inflexible Child

As a therapist, the explanation that I often give parents to describe the workings of this type of child's mind is this: Most people's minds operate like a car. They are heading in a particular direction, but they are looking out the window at all times to make sure the way forward is clear. If they see an obstruction or a detour, if they realize they've missed their turn or taken a wrong turn, they quickly recalibrate and adjust. They are able to respond in the moment in ways that are appropriate to what they see in front of them.

An inflexible child's mind, however, is more like a train. He, too, is heading to a certain destination. However, he is traveling on a track. The rails are pre-set and he cannot veer off of them without disaster ensuing. If he sees something unexpected up ahead, he does not have the capacity to change directions. He can only crash.

Theorists explain this rigidity as a logical, self-protective coping mechanism for some flaw or flaws in the child's sensory processing. Such a child is like someone traveling in the fog; he doesn't clearly perceive what is going on in front of him and around him, and therefore, he needs to stick to the pre-set track upon which he has placed himself. Dealing with all the variables is simply too much for him on a moment-by-moment basis. He needs routine and predictability. Therefore, he resists anything that comes along and pushes him off his course. It "derails" him and he explodes.

All of this adds up to a child who can become very stuck in what he is doing or thinking. He seems mightily willful; interested in getting his own way more than almost anything else in the world. You can offer such a child an incentive in a moment of conflict and he might not even be tempted. He needs to stick to his plan in order to feel safe in his world. In the opening scenario of Yaakov the bookworm, we see this rigidity in action. In his mind, the only way forward was to finish the book. That's what he intended to do, that's what he was trying to do and that's what he *had* to do. When the train tracks were blocked and he couldn't ram his way through, he derailed and exploded.

This "fog" of sensory deficits also explains why such children often fail to respond to social cues. Other people's expressions, tone of voice and body language are simply too subtle to break through. In addition, the same inflexibility that complicates their relationships with the adults in their lives can make them seem oppositional or bossy to other children.

Boruch arrives at the ballfield for a softball game. He likes to pitch.

"O.K., Danny is pitching and Levi is playing first base and Boruch plays second base," says David, the captain.

"I'm pitching," Boruch corrects him.

"Not this time," says David. "Danny will pitch first and then if the game gets close, you'll take over."

"I'm pitching," says Boruch. "I'm not standing around on second base."

David wishes Boruch had been picked for the other team. He's always such a pain.

Boruch doesn't notice that all his teammates are rolling their eyes. He doesn't notice that Danny, the would-be pitcher, is watching expectantly, hoping not to be dethroned. He only knows that his image of today's game was one in which he was the pitcher, not the second baseman.

"Give me the ball," says Boruch. "I'm pitching today."

The tension has already spoiled the fun.

In the opening scenario, another prominent facet of the inflexible personality comes through loud and clear: These children are often hyperlogical. To them, logic is like the railroad track that enables them to stay the course in a world that is difficult to understand. Logic creates a sense of predictability, a precious commodity in their world. Their penchant for logic fuels endless arguments that spark the often-quoted complaint: "For him, everything's an argument."

Knowing all of this is important, even though it will not change your child's nature. That is because with this knowledge, you can understand that your child's challenging behavior is a result of neurological wiring, rather than a *yetzer hara* running rampant. Such children are incapable, in the moment, of shifting gears. They simply lack the equipment. When parents understand this, they usually find their own anger and frustration easier to control. We aren't angry at a baby for crying incessantly until he gets fed; we understand that this is how he survives. Likewise, the inflexible child is trying to survive in a world that seems chaotic to him. He isn't "being stubborn." Rather, he is stuck.

As a side note, some children who exhibit the traits we are discussing in this chapter fall within the definition of Asperger's syndrome. While this is by no means the case across the board, if you have a child who is having difficulty functioning socially or academically due to an inflexible, explosive nature, you might be wise to seek a professional assessment. There may be therapies and resources available to make life far-more tranquil for your child and your family.

Parenting Inflexible Children

We might think that if a child is wired to resist and explode, normal parenting tools go out the window. However, just the opposite is true. The Five-Level tools we have learned will help immensely in bringing these children the structure and the empathy they need to thrive.

In discussing inflexible children, the place to start is Level 5. They need a lot of empathy because oftentimes, it's the only thing that will slow down their forward momentum. Without it, they continue plowing toward the dead end toward which they are heading. They suffer greatly from the feeling, whether dim or acute, that no one really gets them.

Let's look at the opening scenario of Yaakov and his father, Zev, to see how this works. Zev has told Yaakov to get ready to go for a visit to his grandparents, but Yaakov is stuck on the idea that he must finish the last 10 pages of his detective story before he can hit the road. Zev's approach is to give Yaakov logical reasons why his request is unreasonable, which the logic-obsessed Yaakov counters with sound arguments. What else could Zev have done?

"Hi, Yaakov," says Zev. "I see you are reading. Are you at an exciting part of the story?"

"Yeah! I'm right at the end. Pretty soon Detective Duvvy will solve the case!" Yaakov answers.

"Oh, boy, then it's probably going to be very hard for you to put it down now. I know how it bothers you to stop reading so close to the end," says Zev. "I'm sorry we have to get on the road to Zeidy's house right now, but we really do have to go."

"But Daddy! There's just 10 more pages. Can't everyone wait?" Yaakov begs.

"I know you wish we could, but everyone's in their coats ready to go. I'll bet you would love to find out how the story ends before we go. Let's play a game in the car where we try to think up different endings. Then when you finish the book tomorrow, you can see who guessed right."

Here, Zev doesn't try to convince Yaakov that putting the book down is a good idea. Nor does he try to minimize the distress Yaakov feels at being interrupted. Rather, he empathizes with Yaakov's situation and validates his feelings, acknowledging that the child is being asked to do something he finds difficult. This helps Yaakov slow down on the track that is whisking him along to his "finish the book" destination. Once the train slows down, there is some hope of gently switching tracks. Zev has achieved this slowdown not by throwing an obstacle in the way of Yaakov's goal, but by engaging Yaakov's interest in the story: he suggests that the family could try to guess the ending as they drive to the grandparents' house. This way, the father has created a bit of continuity that makes the interruption less abrupt.

Will Yaakov now bend? Perhaps he will or perhaps he will not. He might still stubbornly hold to his insistence that he be allowed to finish the book, despite the father's empathetic approach. As we learned in Level 5, empathy and validation are not enforcement tools. Those are confined to Level 2. However, even if the father must move onto a Level 2 approach, his empathy does its job. It lets Yaakov know that his feelings are valid and understandable. They are simply not going to be the ruling force in this situation.

The Perfect Pre-setting Situation

One Level 2 tool that works very well with the inflexible child's personality is pre-setting behaviors. Such children thrive on the ability to know what's coming; it allows them to set their tracks down in advance and follow them. Even a massive train can easily turn when there is a switch installed in the track. In addition, pre-setting gives such children a sense of control over their environment. Therefore, we can often use pre-setting to preemptively defuse situations that are likely to trigger an explosion.

For example:

It is Wednesday and fish sticks are the main course for dinner that night. Shimmy hates fish sticks. Shimmy's mother tells him before he leaves for school, "Shimmy, I have a little news for you that I know you're not going to like. We've got fish sticks for supper tonight. I know you think they're gross, so I just want to let you know about it ahead of time so you'll be prepared for all that grossness!" She repeats the conversation at 3 p.m. when Shimmy comes home from kindergarten, and then again an hour before dinner. When dinnertime comes Shimmy is completely calm. He's gliding down the tracks that had been laid long in advance.

Five-year-old Moshe is playing with a pile of toys. He often explodes when his toddler brother, Dovid, comes along and swipes his toys away. The children's mother tells Moshe, "In five minutes, Dovid is going to get up from his nap. When I go to get him from his crib, your job is to take your toys, bring them into the den and close the door so that he can't bother you. Are you going to be ready as soon as he gets up?" When Dovid does awaken, Moshe is well prepared. He gathers his toys, makes a grand announcement that he is going to the den, and effortlessly makes the transition.

In the summer months, the Levins put their young children to bed early, before the adults' Shabbos meal. Four-year-old Yosef objects mightily and creates such a ruckus that the parents end up far-more frazzled than if they had let the children stay up for the meal. In an attempt to pre-empt the explosion, Mrs. Levin starts Friday morning to pre-set Yosef's behavior. "Yosef, tonight when Daddy comes home from shul, all the children are going to hear Kiddush and then it's time for bed. Do you understand? Tell Mommy, what are you going to do when Daddy comes home?" Yosef says, "Hear Kiddush and then go to bed."

Mrs. Levin repeats this conversation with her son several times throughout the day. When the father comes home from shul that night, Yosef proudly announces, "I'm going to hear Kiddush and then go to bed."

Often, if you know an upcoming experience will trigger your child but you forgot to pre-set his behavior, you can actually do it retroactively — and at times it still works!

"Oh, no, Shimmy, I forgot to tell you earlier that we're having fish sticks for supper. I meant to tell you this morning before you went to school but I forgot. I'm sorry."

Crystal-Clear Communication

When a child tends to mount loud angry opposition, parents sometimes try to avoid problems by speaking in circles. They express themselves indirectly, partially or through jokes or sarcasm. None of these approaches will accomplish what they parents hope; they will not soften the message and thereby prevent the explosion. In fact, these forms of communication agitate inflexible children. They are already unsteady in their grasp of what is going on around them, what people mean when they speak and what people want from them. If they are confused by what you say, an explosion is not far in coming.

Therefore, we must be very clear, explicit and literal. Spelling out instructions in a step-by-step format helps the child grasp what's being asked of him. It gives him the "clear view" that he so often finds elusive. For example:

- Rather than, "Why are you touching Mommy's keys," say, "Please put the keys down."
- Rather than, "You're upsetting the baby!" say, "Please walk away from the baby."
- Rather than, "Your bus is coming in five minutes," say, "Please go and put your shoes on, take your bag and wait by the door."

Another key application of this idea is breaking down our instructions into components. The process may seem awkward or artificial at first, but you will see that your child is far-more relaxed and comfortable following your directions when you apply this method. For instance:

- Rather than, "Go get into pajamas," say, "Go upstairs. Then open your pajama drawer. Then take out pajama pants and a pajama shirt. Then put them on."
- Rather than, "Clean up the toys," say, "Put the blocks back into the basket. Then put the cars on the shelf. Then make a nice neat pile of the storybooks."
- Rather than, "Come for dinner," say, "Stop your game. Then wash your hands and come to the table."

A three-step instruction is usually the limit for the child to assimilate at once. If there is more to be done, you can give a further three-part instruction after the first three steps are completed.

The value of breaking things down into steps is crucial when we wish to train an inflexible child in Level 3 skills. We can use this method to actually train the child to be more flexible. For example:

"Let's practice the 3-step calm down! You do this when you're starting to feel frustrated and mad when something isn't working the way you want it to:

Number One is to stop what you're doing.

Number Two is to think, *What's another way I can do this?*

And Number Three is to do it!"

Once the child adopts this way of thinking and practices it (often with the help of a chart), he will stick to it. This training lays new tracks that carry the child around the sites of potential derailments rather than leading him to career right into them. The benefits of this training can carry over into all areas of his life.

You may wonder why your perfectly intelligent, albeit explosive, child needs simple tasks to be broken down into so many components. The fact is that for children who are inflexible in their thinking, simple tasks aren't simple. The life skill that makes these tasks self-explanatory for other children is dulled by their sensory deficits. As an example of how this works, imagine a highly intelligent woman — for instance, a research biologist — who is asked to organize her 3-year-old nephew's birthday party. She may be able to name 12-syllable molecules you've never heard of, but she might be at a loss as to what goes into a successful toddler bash. She will need a specific set of instructions, not because she lacks intelligence, but rather, because she lacks a mental map of this particular piece of terrain.

Using the three-step approach, you can familiarize your child with life's many challenging terrains, preparing him to navigate more smoothly. Each child has his own areas that need work and as the parent, it's your job to identify those areas, break them down into concrete steps, and institute Level 3 training programs to address them. Here are some examples:

- Staying calm when things don't go your way;
- Acting flexibly to meet someone else's needs even if they "don't make logical sense" in the child's eyes;
- Time management;
- Staying focused in the presence of distractions;
- Empathy and understanding others;

- Interpreting social cues;
- Taking turns while playing;
- Compromise and problem-solving;
- Anticipating what might go wrong and planning for it;
- Making transitions with flexibility;
- Seeing the gray instead of only black and white;
- Expressing needs, wants and frustrations in words;
- Considering the potential and likely outcomes of their actions.

The conclusion we can draw from here is that when inflexible children fail to comply with adult's wishes, requests and demands, it is usually not because they are being defiant. It is more often because they do not quite perceive what is being asked of them. They feel confused and overwhelmed, and so they explode. Our step-by-step instructions obviate that problem.

One last caveat about communicating with the type of children we are discussing in this chapter: never use sarcasm, hints or double meanings. The child will not get it, but he will feel diminished by it.

Charting Change

Level 3 charts are often a successful tool for inflexible children. In this area, their desire for predictability and order can be utilized toward their own growth. The visible, linear progress toward a reward appeals to them because it is understandable and manageable. They know what is expected and what they have to do to earn the next star on their chart.

Many behavior changes that may seem to require more sophisticated therapies can actually be accomplished by use of charts. For instance, anger and impulse control can improve greatly through charts. Parents can create a chart for "reacting calmly when unpleasant things happen" or "stopping and taking a deep breath when someone teases me." Don't worry about relying upon the child's self-reporting as your source of information; the fact that he is focused on instances throughout the day in which he kept himself calm — no matter how minor the instance — can only help to build that "muscle" in him. As one young client once told me, "Every second that they bothered me I was thinking about the chart. So I just acted calmly and I got my check."

Meeting on Their Turf

A child caught in the rigidity/explosion cycle will try his parents' patience. Because this type of child gets stuck on an idea, he takes a long time to let go. He will pester, repeat himself, nag, noodge and kvetch when other children would have long given up the fight. Empathy is the best response. "Yes, I see how much you want that candy. I wish it were Shabbos so you could have it." "I know how much fun you have playing outside. It's too bad playtime goes by so fast." As many times as they reiterate their desire, you can reiterate your empathy. When you run out of steam, you can turn to your Level 2 tools.

Your child's passion for logical arguments can also be a channel for reaching him. While I generally advise parents to avoid debates with their children, if you yourself are an excellent logician, with these children it sometimes works. But you must make sure that you are taking their logic and arguments seriously. They will not respond to generalized ideas; only if you show them another way from the inside of their argument itself will they be able to acknowledge your point. If they really can see the logic of your argument, their natures may compel them to give in. On the other hand, they may feel trapped and confused by your superior argument, which can trigger a blowup. In that case, it's time to back off and return to your other approaches.

The message I hope to impart in this chapter is twofold: First of all, children who are wired like this cannot help the way they respond. They are the way Hashem created them (just as we all are), and they require validation, affection and support no less, and perhaps more, than other children. Secondly, they also require boundaries like all other children, and the fact that they can behave in temperamental, seemingly unmanageable ways does not negate our obligation to set those boundaries. Neither does it mean that they are incapable of learning to respect boundaries. We can raise them with love and security, self-esteem and life skills, using the same tools we use for all our children. It only takes a willingness to understand what the world looks like through their eyes.

Teaching Truthfulness

You walk into the kitchen and find a half-gallon of ice cream sitting on the counter turning into soup, and a drippy ice-cream scoop lying next to it. You call out to the general public in your household, "Who took out ice cream and didn't put it away?"

Despite the fact that all your children are in earshot, there's no answer. You ask again, this time with some agitation in your voice. Again, there's no confessions forthcoming.

Now you're really getting upset, because not only did someone waste a pricey half-gallon of premium chalav Yisrael ice cream, but someone is lying…or at least failing to answer truthfully.

What would break this deadlock? What would get the wrongdoer to come forward readily and avoid the need for an inquisition?

Leaving aside the question of whether it is necessary or helpful to demand confessions as the parent above has done, let's just take the scenario as is, and imagine a way to encourage truthfulness in the children.

"Whoever left it out, I want you to come and tell me. I'm not angry. No one's going to get punished."

If you are a parent reading this, you might think, *What? How does that teach the child to be more responsible? I'd tell the whole bunch of them that I'm not buying any more ice cream until someone tells me who did this!*

You may be right that this approach doesn't create a consequence that would ensure that more care be taken in the future. What it does accomplish, however, is something much more important. The child will tell the truth. The child will become accustomed to telling the truth rather than training himself in deceit and evasion to avoid consequences. The value of this trait cannot be overstated.

Nine-year-old Boruch is spending a summer at a well-known, well-respected overnight camp. One day during rest hour, his bunkmate invites him to walk with him to his "secret hideout" in a nearby patch of woods. When they get to the secluded spot, the bunkmate reaches under his T-shirt and pulls out a comic book he's hidden.

"You gotta see this! It's so cool!" he tells Boruch.

The material is contraband, and for good reason. The graphic illustrations of various superheroes include female characters dressed in immodest outfits that make the more innocent Boruch squirm. He wants to run, but he feels foolish. He knows that lots of boys read comic books and he doesn't want to appear naïve. So he looks on with his bunkmate until finally, he's able to say, "Let's get back. It's almost time for swimming!"

In a situation like this, a child's heart is roiling with a molten mixture of emotions. He's ashamed of what he's seen and done, yet he's worried about fitting in with his peers. At the same time, he may have enjoyed the taste of forbidden fruit. He's also worried: *Am I going off the derech? Am I bad?*

This is a tremendous load for a child to carry alone. At this critical juncture, if he can talk the situation out with his parents, he can avoid untold troubles. However, if he feels that his parents cannot handle the information, that they will become angry, agitated or dramatically disappointed, or that they'll impose some dire consequence like driving up to camp and taking him home, they will not be, in the child's mind, part of any solution to his dilemma. They will instead be another facet of the dilemma: *I've got this problem, that problem, another problem and on top of it all, if my parents find out, I've got an even worse problem.*

As our children grow and interact more with people outside our homes, the potential for dangerous situations expands. Those to whom we entrust our children may not always be trustworthy. As we have sadly discovered, there are adults who are not mentally healthy or morally sound, which may leave our children subject to exploitation or abuse. A child who knows that he has a clear and open line to his parents is protected from the worst of these situations. He can immediately seek help, process what has occurred and avoid further abuse. We hear of cases that have gone on for years, in which a child is a virtual prisoner of a sick individual, and *secrecy is the only lock on that prison door.*

Even within the realm of normal, the experiences, options and information available to our children today are far too numerous for them to handle. Parents often do not even know what kind of images, music and ideas are entering their world from the media that have infiltrated every corner of society. Emotionally and spiritually, this proliferation of influences can do grave damage if there are not trusted adults in the children's lives to help them put things into the proper perspective.

Even without the input of popular culture, the news alone can wreak internal havoc. What are children to think about nuclear arms being built by countries dedicated to the destruction of Eretz Yisrael, or fanatics running rampant, kidnaping and beheading people across the Mideast? How are they to understand the illness and suffering of good people? Where do they find Hashem in all of this? How do they understand *Hashgachah Pratis*? They are bound to have doubts.

These are questions far too vital to our children's developing spirituality to be left to chance. But they will not tell us what's on their minds if in doing so, they will be subjecting themselves to negative consequences for having seen or heard something forbidden to them, or thinking thoughts we have identified as bad.

Finally, a shaky hold on the *middah* of truthfulness is devastating to healthy emotional development and interpersonal relationships. If a person is not who they seem to be, he never feels that others value him for who he really is. His relationships feel false and hollow. Such a person lives life alone, even if he is surrounded by legions of friends and family. He is ever fearful that others will somehow find out what's really going on inside him.

The Rule for Encouraging Truth-telling

As we see, honesty is not just a matter of being willing to 'fess up and take the consequences of one's actions. It's one of the essential traits we must strive to develop in our children. Therefore, the rule for dealing with issues of truth and falsehood is this:

Whenever a child chooses to tell the truth regarding something about which he might have been tempted to lie, there should be NO consequences for the wrongdoing.

Our one and only goal in these situations is to encourage and reward truthfulness. To do so, we must take away the incentive for lying. There will be times when this means temporarily putting aside a Level 2 or Level 3 goal.

For instance, let's suppose that in the opening scenario, the children are often irresponsible with the food they serve themselves. The parents have had to throw away numerous containers of spoiled milk, to clean up spills, wash used dishes, sweep up crumbs and so forth. Therefore, they have instituted a family rule: the kitchen is off-limits except for two pre-set snack times. Furthermore, there is a rotation of children in charge of making sure the kitchen is cleaned up at the end of snack time.

With that as a backdrop, the mother walks into the kitchen to find the melted ice cream. Someone has broken the rule and taken a snack on "off-hours." Based on everything we have learned until this point, we would say that consistency demands that there be a consequence for breaking that rule. And of course, first the mother must find out who broke it.

So how does the mother remain consistent and yet open a pathway for the child who ate the ice cream to tell the truth? At this point, she must choose truthfulness over consistency because the top priority is to promote honesty. Nevertheless, the rule for snacking still stands. The concept is comparable to being *mechalel*

Shabbos to tend to a medical emergency. The fact that we may do so does not in any way abrogate the laws of Shabbos observance; it simply indicates that potentially irrevocable damage to a human life must be avoided, even on Shabbos.

Given this imperative of promoting honesty, parents might be tempted to use honey to get the truth and then change gears once they find out what has happened. For example, the camper, Boruch, calls his parents and sounds very low. They beg him to tell them what's wrong, urging him to trust them and turn to them in his time of need. "We won't be mad," they promise. Then, when he tells them about the comic book, they say, "That's it. This camp is no place for you. We're coming to get you."

"But you said you wouldn't be mad!" the child counters.

"We're not mad at *you*, Boruch," they reason. "But we can't let you stay in a place where the counselors don't even know what's going on. We're doing this because we love you!"

It will be a long, long time before Boruch ever again trusts his parents with sensitive information. There is no way that being removed from camp and dragged back to the hot, friendless city will seem to be anything but a punishment for him.

The parents might, however, work behind the scenes to ensure that the scenario doesn't repeat itself. They might alert the counselor or the camp director to the situation so that they can deal with the boy who has brought the contraband into camp. Even then, it would be important to ensure that the boy doesn't detect that Boruch told on him, potentially sentencing Boruch to the even worse fate of being ostracized from his bunk. The exact strategy the parents should follow is not the point here; what matters is that Boruch can tell his parents what happened and *nothing* negative will happen to him as a result.

Inspiring Honesty

On the other side of the coin, we should praise truth-telling to the heavens. Whenever a child deals honestly with a difficult truth, we should not take it for granted that "of course" he knows that lying is wrong. Rather, we should acknowledge his courage. "I know it must be hard for you to tell me this, and I'm very proud that you did it." Using Level 3 praising techniques (TASC) we can solidify our children's allegiance to the truth.

Level 4 stories and inspiration are another way to reinforce the value of truth. There are so many stories of people whose honesty and integrity were legendary, for whom even the slightest misstatement was abhorrent. We can further instill in our children the goal of becoming a trusted and trustworthy person. There are those with whom others trusted their fortunes, their secrets, their businesses and much more. We want to encourage our children to strive to become such people. While greatness in many other areas may be more dependent on natural gifts and talents, greatness in honesty is available to everyone.

Personal example is of course paramount. We all have heard the cautionary tale of the parent who reprimands his child for lying and then, moments later, when the phone rings, instructs the child, "Tell him I'm not home." Instructing a child to lie is an obvious negative model: "Say you're 10 so we don't have to pay full price for your ticket." There are more subtle signals as well. For instance, if a parent tells the child that he will receive a certain reward — or even a consequence — and then doesn't come through with it, the message is that we are not bound by our words.

On the other hand, parents have wonderful opportunities to display their high regard for honesty and truth. They can openly refuse to take part in *"shtik"* that has a taint of dishonesty, give truthful answers even when they are not convenient, pay the full price for their short, skinny 12-year-old even though he could pass for 10 and so forth. In all these matters, parents can and should point out that, "I want to tell the *emes*. It's worth the extra money (time, trouble, etc.) to be truthful."

Dealing With Lies

Despite your efforts to make honesty a win-win proposition for your children, you might find that they sometimes fall short. At times, their aim is not even to get away with wrongdoing. They might embellish a story to make themselves look more heroic or just to make the story more interesting. At a young age, falsehood might be a case of "magical thinking" in which the child is not yet mature enough to fully distinguish between what he wishes would be and what really is. In all these cases, the best advice is to refrain from panicking and trust that, as the child matures and his understanding of truth deepens, these behaviors will stop.

In a child's day-to-day life, the issue of lying should not arise often. Because we do not want truth to become a constant issue, try to avoid setting the child up for a fall. Don't ask, "What just happened?" when you saw exactly what happened. If you see your child grab a toy away from his sibling, simply state, "I saw

Dovid take Yossi's fire truck," and deal with it through a Level 2 consequence. By avoiding incriminating questions to which you already know the answer, you avoid giving your children the opportunity to lie. Some typical questions that are aimed at gaining a confession rather than information (assuming you already know the answer) include:

- Who broke this?
- Where do you think you're going?
- Why did your rebbi call me today?
- How did those cookie crumbs get in your bed?
- Who started the fight?

In all these cases, if the parent already knows the answer, he should not ask. If he does not know the answer, he will not be able to ascertain the truthfulness of whatever answer he is given. Therefore, asking provides little or no benefit, while giving the children a tempting opportunity to lie and cast blame on each other.

If you don't already know what happened, then you may have to ask a question that opens a possibility of a response that is half-true or not true at all. However, assuming that you have adopted the "tell the truth and you don't get punished" rule, there should be very few instances in which your children will tell you an outright lie.

For some children, however, the admission of any fault or guilt is too much; to them, someone else is always at fault. Most of the time, the best strategy, if possible, is to deal with the underlying wrongdoing and overlook the lie or denial.

Six-year-old Rochel is playing with her older sister Devorah, dressing a porcelain doll that Devorah has received for her birthday. Rochel grabs the doll.

"Let's put her in her Shabbos clothes," Rochel says as she begins stuffing the doll's limbs into a miniature lace dress.

"No, it's time for her to go to sleep," says Devorah. "Give her back to me. I want to put her in her nightgown."

"No!" Rochel insists. "I already have one sleeve on. Let me finish."

Stating, "It's my doll," Devorah grabs it back, but Rochel hangs on. In the tug of war, the lace dress rips.

Rochel knows she is in trouble. She was grabbing her sister's doll and trying to dictate how it would be dressed, and now the dress was ruined.

"Devorah ripped her new doll's dress!" Rochel runs to tell her mother, hoping to deflect blame. However, the mother has seen the entire incident.

"We're not allowed to grab other people's toys. Now the dress is ruined. You'll have to buy the doll a new dress with some of your Chanukah money," the mother says.

In this case, it is enough for the mother to deal with the little girl's appropriation of her sister's doll and the resulting damage it caused. She does not have to begin an interrogation: "Devorah ripped the dress? Who really ripped the dress?" Nor does she have to impose a consequence for the child's fib, such as a timeout for "not saying the *emes*."

The time for dealing with lying as an issue of its own is when it becomes the child's default mode or a frequent occurrence. In that case, parents can handle lying in the same way as they would handle any Level 2 behavior that they want to curtail. If the parent *knows the child is lying,* he should simply say, "That's not the *emes.* Time-out." The sequence of events should be straight and clear: false statement, time-out. The sequence includes no lecture on the value of truth or the evil of dishonesty. The approach is strictly behavioral: "When I don't tell the truth, this is what happens to me." It is no different than, "When I touch something hot, I get burned."

The temptation to turn such an event into a teaching moment might be very great, because after all, we're teaching our children one of the pillars of morality and spirituality. This is where your understanding of Five-Level Parenting becomes essential. You now know that pillars of morality and spirituality cannot be taught through negative consequences, but only through inspiration and role-modeling. As we noted earlier, truthfulness is a prime lesson for Level 4 techniques. On the contrary, getting a child caught up in a dynamic of accusations and punishments for lies casts this crucial trait in an oppressive, gray tone. *Emes* should be a bright beacon toward which our children run, not a quagmire in which they get trapped.

On the rare occasions in which *emes* becomes the subject of a consequence, there is one screaming warning sign parents must heed: Do not proceed unless you know for a fact that your child actually lied. Follow the Torah's directive to "judge others in accordance with merit." In other words, always give the benefit of the doubt. Ask yourself:

- Did I see what happened?
- Did I hear what happened?
- If I am relying on someone else's report, is that person reliable?
- Does that person have an axe to grind?

- Am I basing my assumptions solely on the child's past actions or personality, when this time, he may *not* have done wrong?

It's so easy to blame a difficult child for being difficult yet again. Since certain behaviors are within his repertoire, we can easily imagine that he has done whatever he is being accused of doing, and that his denial is a self-protective lie. We may be right, but we may be wrong.

"Levi hit me!" cries Shimon.

"Levi, if you hit once more, you're going to time-out," says Mom.

"But I didn't hit him!" Levi protests.

Levi has the self-restraint of Mount Vesuvius. He is constantly fighting with his siblings. Ninety percent of all family disruptions can be traced to his tempestuous little heart.

"That's not the emes, Levi. It's bad enough to hit, but then to lie about it too! Go to time-out right now!"

Imagine if Levi really had not hit his brother. It's possible. His mother did not see the incident happen. Shimon, the eager witness, is far from objective. In fact, in this family, all the children know that when trouble is brewing, they can blame it on Levi and be fairly certain that they will be believed.

In this scenario, two grave injuries have been dealt to Levi. First of all, he has been falsely accused. His protests are not even entertained for a moment. He is guilty without trial, guilty by virtue of his personality and track record. Because these are things he cannot change, his hope of improving himself is crushed. He has no way to start a clean slate.

If, on this particular occasion, he had actually restrained himself, actually held himself back when he really felt like hitting

Shimon, his effort would now appear futile. If Shimon had provoked him just to set him off and watch the fireworks, then Levi would feel defeated and humiliated by his mother's instant defense of Shimon.

Secondly, Levi has been painted as a liar. His protests received no credence whatsoever. The mother was telling him, "It doesn't matter what you say. I know you're lying."

If we place these risks on one side of a scale and on the other side, place the risk of Levi getting away with hitting his brother, we quickly see that in a case where there's any room for doubt, parents should not make assumptions. On one side of the scale, we have a child who may be suffering the devastating effects of a false accusation and the knowledge that he is seen as a liar. On the other side, we have a ruckus that the mother could resolve in any number of other ways, some of which are: She can ignore it, she can validate both of them or she can send them to play in different rooms. But even if she can't do anything, she doesn't really know what happened, and therefore, accusations of lying should never enter the picture.

This brings us to the second screaming warning sign when dealing with issues of *emes*: Never characterize your child as a liar. Somehow, despite every caution from the worlds of Torah, *chinuch* and psychology, we persist in thinking that if we paste a terrible label on a child, he will do everything in his power to shed that label. We think that if we say, "You're lazy," the child will rise up to prove he's not lazy. We think that if we say, "That's *goyish*," he will drop what he's doing, singing, wearing, etc., to prove that he is indeed a Jew through and through. That is what we think.

However, what we know is that the opposite is true. The child will own the label and live up to it.

This rule of human nature is a powerful reason to keep any Level 2 interactions over *emes* issues as neutral as possible. If you feel that there is a real issue with *emes*, which needs to be addressed, impose the consequence in reference to the child's action only, not his *middos*. "You didn't say the *emes*," is all that needs to be said.

To summarize what we've discussed here, we can foster honesty and truthfulness in our children in these ways:

- Let them know that if they tell the truth, they will not be punished for any wrongdoing they've revealed. Then stick to that guarantee once the truth is out.
- Praise them for telling the truth, even if what they've told you is not praiseworthy in itself.
- Overlook self-protective fibbing as much as possible and deal directly with the behavior itself.
- Use Level 2 consequences only when dishonesty is becoming a habit and getting in the way of their development.
- Use Level 2 only when you know **beyond a doubt** that your child is not telling the truth.
- In imposing consequences for lying, do not lecture about the beauty of truthfulness or the evil of lying. Just call out the behavior and respond to it.
- Never label your child a liar, either directly or by implication.
- Inspire your child to admire truthfulness through stories, learning and most of all, your own example.

By using these strategies, we can raise children who possess a firm grasp on one of the most precious traits a person can have. At the close of *Shemoneh Esrei* each day, we pray for Hashem to protect us from speaking deceitfully. Only from a position of *emes* can we reach out to Him and reach out to each other, giving and receiving, loving and serving from the real, true essence of our souls.

It's Not Working!

*F*ive-year-old Temmy is a terror at the Shabbos table. She sits next to her brother and purposely bumps his arm as he's eating his chicken soup. The soup spills, the boy yells and the mother, having seen exactly what happened, sends Temmy to time-out.

Temmy doesn't budge as her mother counts to three. The mother wants to sit at the Shabbos table with her family and enjoy the meal, but instead, she must get up, take Temmy firmly by the hand and practically drag her off to her time-out spot in the adjacent den.

Temmy comes out of the room seconds later. "I'm not in time-out!" she announces defiantly. The mother drags her back in, closes the door and stands there holding it shut while the rest of the family digs into their piping-hot main course.

Temmy screams and kicks at the door while the mother wonders what she is really gaining with this "time-out business." She can't help but imagine that one solid whack would have solved the problem more efficiently.

Many of the parents I counsel, like Temmy's mother, think that because they still face challenges in disciplining and dealing with their children, the Five-Level Parenting system doesn't work. But let's look at this from a different perspective: A person adopts a new eating plan to lose weight and become healthier. Would he expect his plan to bring him to his ideal weight on week one? Obviously not, and yet we may well expect our parenting plan to yield such instant results. The new eating plan does, however, immediately set its users on the path to a healthy weight. If they use the plan day after day, assess how it is working periodically and make adjustments as needed, it will indeed get them where they want to go. The same can be said of this parenting plan.

Therefore, the first question to ask yourself if you feel that "it's not working" is whether you are using this plan as a long-term program or a magic bullet. As a long-term program, reassessments and readjustments are to be expected. Turning once again to the diet metaphor, what if you weigh yourself at the end of the first week and discover that, despite following the diet exactly, you haven't lost a pound? You would realize then that you need to adjust your food intake or your energy output. That's not "not working." It's revealing necessary information that lets you know how your plan works with your individual metabolism. Likewise, the problems that persist when you begin using this program reveal for you how the various techniques work with your individual family dynamics. You may discover that the goals you've designated or the tools you are using need adjustment.

Therefore, a key to using this program effectively is assessment and planning. Sit down once a month or even every two weeks and take stock of how the system is working for you. Look at all five levels, all the goals you have set for the present, and assess whether or not you are moving in the right direction. Ask yourself:

- Have I defined the challenges correctly and identified reasonable goals?
- What situations are being helped by the tools I'm using? Which seem to be as challenging as or more challenging than they were when we started?
- Should we reduce or change some of our goals?
- Should we add new goals? If so, which tools should we use to achieve them? Within what level do these goals fall?

This review should not take more than a half-hour. By investing this small amount of time, you'll be helping to keep your own efforts on track and refresh your enthusiasm for instituting change in your parenting style. Otherwise, default mode is bound to kick in and Five-Level Parenting, with all its tremendous potential to enhance sanity, stability and love in your home, may be relegated to the "been there, done that" pile.

What Do You Expect?

To be sure, most parents who seek help in their parenting methods have one powerful motivation in common: things appear to be out of control. They get no peace, no cooperation and as a result, very little joy out of their parenting role. They know they need to fix the situation. The mistake many parents make is to believe that "fixed" means that their children will behave like little robots, fulfilling their parents' requests and obeying their rules without a moment's resistance.

Not only is that not the outcome of this method, it is not the goal, either. In three levels out of the five, obedience is not even an issue. Level 3 is about training in lifelong behavioral patterns habits; Level 4 is about inspiring children to cherish our values, and Level 5 is about nurturing their emotional health by building their trust in themselves and the world around them. All of these levels are aimed at creating an environment where children *choose* to do the right thing so that they can grow in a holistic, grounded fashion. That's because one of the key differences between successful and unsuccessful adults is "Knowing the consequences, can you decide on your own to make a choice in your best interests? Or do you ignore those longer-term consequences and go for the immediate reward?"

If we as parents set the consequences and let the child "figure it out by himself" that his immediate gratification isn't worth it, we are giving them the opportunity to practice this behavior of acting in their own long-term interests.

In using this system, those parents who succeed are putting at least as much effort into these three levels as they put into Levels 1 and 2. In doing so, they foster internally driven growth that generates true self-esteem and *simchah*. If our goal is only obedience, we might be able to achieve it for now, but a child who feels bossed and controlled is at risk of seeking to shed those shackles as soon as he is able. He is likely to harbor resentment that festers until eventually, when his parents no longer have control of him, it bubbles to the surface.

But what about Level 2? What about Temmy's mother? Where is the sanity that time-out is supposed to deliver? Here, too, expectations are a key factor. The goal in Level 2 is to create a clearly defined set of boundaries in the child's life. The more consistent we are with these boundaries and the less emotional we are about enforcing them, the sooner our children will come to view them as "the way the world works." Depending on a child's temperament, this perspective can take longer or less time to achieve, but ultimately, it makes a tremendous impact on the functioning of a household and the manageability of our children. Most importantly, it creates a secure and stable world for them.

Level 2 does not, however, ensure perfect obedience. That is because we are dealing with human beings. They can feel unusually tired or cranky, they can be ill, they can have grievances or worries of which we are unaware. While these situations are not usually a reason to abandon the boundaries we have set, they can explain why children may be uneven in their ability to abide by those boundaries. We might feel we've licked a problem and then see it crop up again. Sometimes we may have to work harder than usual to keep our children within bounds. This is to be expected and does not signify failure. However, if a parent is aiming at total control of his children with no variation in the script, the Five-Level Parenting method will not deliver.

All You Need Is Love?

As unproductive as it is to pour all our effort into Level 2 and let the other "touchy-feely" parts of parenting take care of themselves, the opposite approach is also bound to fail. Some parents love so much to play with their kids, buy them treats, take them on outings and see them smile and laugh that they resist doing anything to ruin the party. Some parents are so busy and distracted that as long as the children are not actively bothering them, bothering each other or heading into danger, they resist rocking the boat. In both cases, the parents' motto might be "Let them be. They're happy."

When this is the case, the only Level 2 tool being used is "do nothing," while the other Level 2 tools falls by the wayside. For instance, the children are up way past their bedtime every night, they are always tired in school, but they're playing happily. "Let them be." Or they should be doing their homework but instead, they are playing Hide-and-Seek with the neighborhood kids. Rather than having to put out the energy it will take to get them inside and started on their homework, the mother lets it slide. The peace in the house gives her a chance to get some chores done; why ruin it?

Rather than moving into a more active Level 2 response, these parents might think that they will discuss the situation later with their children and encourage better cooperation for the future. They rely on the children's understanding of the issue, their ability to perceive that their lapses cost them in sleep or school performance, and to act on that perception. The only problem is that this will never happen. It would be the rare child who would put away her book or game thinking, *I better get to sleep or I'll be tired tomorrow in school.*

Parents who try to skate past the Level 2 situations do their children a grave disservice. It's the parents' consistency that helps the child develop true self-discipline, which is a key to success in life and stability within. Children are not born with a sense of boundaries and obligations. In fact, the opposite is true. They are naturally untamed and demanding, a feature that can clearly be seen in children who are spoiled by their parents. If they never experience immediate and consistent boundaries, they cannot learn the skill of putting aside what they *feel* like doing in order to do what they *have* to do. Sadly, for someone without this skill, life unfolds in a disastrous manner.

Furthermore, if we do not maintain our boundaries and rules, we may not be able to maintain our cool, either. Most parents are not as "laid back" as they might believe themselves to be. Instead they just operate on a nice, long fuse. Eventually, the conflict and chaos, the mess and sleeplessness, the absence of any schedule, order or privacy burns the fuse down to the end and the parent explodes. Such parents may wonder why, after "I've explained a million times" or "discussed it with him nicely already" that their children persist in misbehaving. The reason is that they are children. They cannot be expected to alter their behavior significantly based on explanations and discussions. In truth, even adults have difficulty refraining from harmful habits just because they heard, read or learned that they should do so.

For all these reasons, parents who shy away from Level 2 interactions are bound to find that the system is not living up to its promise. They may be so mired in the "administrative details" of running their home that they have little time or energy for big-picture goals like inspiring their children and spending quality time with them.

What Do You Expect of Your Child?

When parents are putting substantial effort into all five levels of this program and yet coming up short of expectations, the most common reason is that they are not accurately assessing what their child is capable of accomplishing. This can be the case particularly in Level 3.

If you are trying to train your child in a new skill or routine and find that your program isn't getting anywhere, you may not be communicating your instructions in a way that the child is capable of following. As we discussed earlier in this chapter with regard to inflexible children, what seems like a simple instruction to us can be confusing to a child, just by virtue of his inexperience. Even a child who does not display an unusual amount of rigidity often needs procedures to be broken down into bite-size components in order to follow through with the task.

"Tonight is the first night of our 'getting ready for bed' chart," Mom *says in her cheerleader voice. "Are you ready, Avi?"*

"Yeah! I'm gonna get a star and pretty soon I'll have a whole line of stars and then I'm gonna get a remote control car!" says 5-year-old Avi. He's on board.

"O.K., it's 7:30. Time to get ready for bed!" Mom chirps. She sets about washing dishes while Avi heads upstairs.

Fifteen minutes later, Avi has not yet appeared in his pajamas, as he was supposed to do. "Avi, what are you doing up there?" Mom calls out.

"I'm getting into my pajamas," he answers.

She goes back to kitchen cleanup and another 10 minutes go by. It's almost bedtime and Avi still hasn't appeared. She goes upstairs to see what's happening. Avi is sitting on the floor, dressed in tzitzis and pajama pants, flipping through a storybook.

"What happened, Avi?" Mom asks. "Why aren't you in your pajamas?"

"I couldn't find my fire-truck shirt," he explains. *"Do I still get a star?"*

In the above scenario, Avi was ready and willing, but not able, to follow the instruction "get ready for bed." He got lost along the way and then became distracted with his book. What the mother had anticipated would be a 10-minute self-propelled procedure stretched into a 35-minute mother-assisted procedure that accomplished nothing toward teaching Avi how to perform his bedtime routine efficiently on his own.

What went wrong? Avi is only 5 and this is the first time he is ever going to get ready for bed on his own. He simply does not know what steps he has to take. To make a success out of this Level 3 training program, the mother needs to break down "get ready for bed" into Avi-size steps.

1. Go upstairs and open your top drawer. Take out your pajama pants.

2. Open your second drawer and find your pajama shirt.

3. Take off your clothes and put them in the hamper.

4. Put on your pajamas.

Similarly, certain behaviors we desire to teach may be too broad for a child to grasp. If that's the case, we need to break them down into "microskills" that are clearly defined and doable. For example, if we want to train our child to get along better with his siblings, we will have to teach him a variety of individual skills which comprise the overall goal of "getting along." These include:

1. Sharing toys

2. Dealing with someone cheating

3. Dealing with being hit or pushed

4. Responding to teasing

5. Taking turns

5. Speaking nicely.

Each of these skills can be taught as its own separate achievement with its own chart and rewards. For two weeks, a child may work on nothing but keeping his cool when teased. Once one habit is ingrained, you can introduce the next step.

As you review your progress with your Five-Step Parenting plan, you might discover that some of these skills need to be broken down even further. *Your child will teach you what he needs.* Through his behavior, you'll be able to see what he has managed to grasp. If you see that he's still "not getting it" in some area, break it down further. If you see that he's quite capable of doing more, you can demand more. For instance, you can make a chart for "keeping calm when someone isn't nice to me." That encompasses several microskills, yet some children will be able to perform at this level.

A mismatch of parents' expectations and children's abilities can also emerge at Level 2. If these tools are not working well for you, the reason might be that your child is not developmentally able to do what you are demanding of him. Sometimes children do not yet have the self-control to respond as you want them to. For instance, a child snatches a cookie right before dinner and you tell him, "Put the cookie down and we'll save it for dessert." A 3-year-old might have real difficulty putting that cookie down. You might start counting to three, but the child still doesn't respond because he doesn't have it in him to release that cookie. You may look at this situation and think, *Time-out doesn't work.*

However, the problem is not with time-out as a technique; it is with the expectation that the child will have the necessary self-control to do what is being demanded.

If you find yourself using time-out often, your child is teaching you something: "You're demanding too much of me." For children who are too young, too immature or too willful to bend to this method, parents can use a Level 2 tool that demands less from the child instead. Often the best, quickest and most efficient move is to physically intercede. In the case of the child with the cookie, the mother can simply take the cookie away from the child and put it in an unreachable spot. "That's where we will keep it until after dinner," she can say. The child might cry and complain, but the boundary has been maintained.

Level 2 sometimes fails because parents don't have the energy to follow through. As we've noted elsewhere in this book, if you hope to intercede in your child's behavior by remote control, while still working on your computer, immersed in your learning, working in the kitchen, talking on the phone, feeding the baby or even taking your Shabbos nap, you will not succeed. Your child knows that you don't want to stop what you are doing to deal with him. He knows you will just yell directions from your place and hope for the best. If he's lucky, you'll give up. If he's unlucky, you'll experience enough annoyance to produce a surge of adrenalin that will finally propel you onto the scene, most likely in a state of anger.

When assessing how to use Level 2 tools effectively, your child is your guide. What works and what doesn't, and why? Is he capable of doing what you're asking? How can you tweak your approach to better suit your child's temperament and level of maturity? Once again, your child is your best source of information.

Things Were Going Great and Then...

As in many areas of life, progress in parenting can be expected to come in fits and starts. You might succeed in helping your child to adopt a new habit, behavior or attitude and gratefully cross that goal off your to-do list when all of a sudden, the child seems to backtrack. This should not be surprising, as we all experience this constant battle between our old bad habits and our inspiration to do better. Inspiration is a notoriously slippery substance, even when backed by positive actions. For instance, how many people quit smoking, truly enjoy all the benefits of their new status, but then slip back into their old habit? How many people lose weight by eating with great self-control for months, and then gain it all back? Consistency is hard to come by.

However, we can train a child in consistency. This is done in Level 3 with a program that awards consistent performance. For instance, a child may get a star for each night he does his homework right after school. To earn a prize, he must get five stars in a row. This type of training program gives the child motivation to do the same thing day after day, knowing that if on Day 4 he decides, "Forget it, I'll be good tomorrow," then he is back to square one.

As we mentioned earlier, inconsistent performance might also come from a special circumstance. If your child is not doing what he has already learned to do, you might find that there is a reason. The overall point is that setbacks do not mean that there's no real progress.

Misuses of Level 2

In our discussion about the Level 4 goal of teaching values, we compared Level 2 to a steam shovel. It is meant to clear away the rocks and thistles so that the parents can build the edifice of their child's personality. We noted that you can't build with a steam shovel; you can only destroy. This is an important concept to reiterate when we are discussing the overall efficacy of Five-Level Parenting. We cannot and should not try to teach our children *anything* with Level 2, except that certain actions have certain consequences.

When parents embellish their Level 2 interactions with preaching or explanations, this tool loses its potency. Rules and consequences, intervention and time-out are only meant to clear the field of obstacles so that the real teaching can go on in the higher-level interactions. The temptation to teach a child a lesson as you move to enforce your boundaries must be resisted. These are not teachable moments; rather, they are meant to be totally bland and unemotional. The only message the child needs to receive in a Level 2 interaction is "This is what happens in our family when I…"

As a side benefit to consistent use of Level 2, your child will no doubt develop a certain amount of self-discipline. He will come to realize that there are certain things he must do and certain things he should never do. As in the "hot stove" analogy, the consistent result will be enough to motivate him — no commentary necessary -- to "choose" to avoid the unpleasant consequence. Even though the children's sense of security and self-worth benefits greatly from firm boundaries, the parents' only real goal with Level 2 should be to ensure healthy, productive routines, sanity and stability in their home.

Reassessing the Higher Goals

As we move up the ladder to the higher goals of spiritual and emotional health, our success depends on keeping a "finger on the pulse" of our children's lives. Their needs change. As they get older, sometimes they want less one-on-one time because they are more interested in being with their friends or engaging in their own pursuits. On the other hand, sometimes they may need more time. Perhaps they are having trouble adjusting to a new phase of life, or something is troubling them.

They change, and as they do, we have to readjust our relationship with them. What inspires an 8-year-old might earn an eye roll from a 10-year-old. A decision we insist on making for a young child — such as what to wear or eat — might be reasonably entrusted to an older child. Knowing when and how to begin letting go is one of the great challenges of parenthood.

We also have to keep reminding ourselves that they are not us. They may respond very differently to life than we do. The father who finds *gematria* fascinating may have a son who finds it uninspiring and would much rather learn a *halachah* at the Shabbos table. This is not a rejection of the father's *chinuch*. A mother who loves to bake and wants to share that with her daughter might find that her daughter would much rather play piano. This is not a rejection of the mother's companionship. Just as we are not our parents, our children are not us. In every way, our goal is to help them become the healthiest, happiest and holiest version of *who they are*.

Taking Our Own Temperature

Finally, in attempting to assess how well the Five-Level Parenting plan is working for you, your own emotional state is an important guide. One of the fundamental purposes of this plan is to provide tools that parents can trust to help them stay in control of their households, thus reducing the amount of anger and frustration spewing forth into the home. Therefore, the big questions are, "Are we getting angry less often? Are we getting angry more often? What situations still end up provoking anger?" The answers to those questions will teach you a great deal about what remains to be done.

Any interpersonal relationship is a complicated dance between two individuals, who are in fact two entire worlds in and of themselves. When you take into account the interactions of two parents and a brood of children, all of different ages, stages and personalities, the complexity of the equation is probably impossible to quantify. The only way to handle that complexity is to have a GPS: a destination and a plan for getting there. But even with a good GPS, you sometimes take a wrong turn. Then it's time to recalibrate. That means the GPS *is* working.

What Not to Do

In the previous chapters of this book, we have explored useful tools for achieving our goals as parents of healthy, happy, spiritually and emotionally sound Jewish children. By the process of elimination, the reader can deduce that any tools we have not included in those chapters have not proven to be useful tools. However, these excluded practices are not just ineffective. They are often dangerous. We have touched upon some of these dangers already, but in this chapter, we will spell out clearly, with all the cautions and warning labels, what tools *not* to use in the course of raising our children.

Don't # 1: Shock and Awe

There is one place for scaring a child out of his behavior, and that is at Level 1. There, we want to establish a firm, negative association with a dangerous behavior: a behavior that, if repeated, might do irrevocable harm to the child or some other person such as a friend or sibling. Unless we are trying to protect life and limb, there is no constructive purpose to inflicting pain and fear (we are not talking about fear as in reverence and awe, but rather as in fear of harm).

First of all, if we waste our sharp reprimands and *potches* on spilled milk, messy rooms, bedtime balkiness or other typical childrearing challenges, they lose their ability to get our children's attention. In that case, we lose our most powerful tool for preventing the most devastatingly damaging situations. When running out into the street elicits the same response as fighting over a toy, the child will not be able to perceive the urgency of the first situation. Furthermore, if these harsh reactions are commonplace, the child may eventually cease to be jarred or frightened by his parent's response. Therefore, there will be no high-impact impression to stop him from repeating his dangerous act in the future.

We know that a child will not touch a hot stove twice. The reason is clear; he doesn't want to get burned twice. He associates the stove with pain and his basic survival instinct tells him to avoid it in the future. However, most children cannot conceive of the pain they could G-d forbid encounter by running into the street or playing with matches because they do not experience it firsthand. The parent's Level 1 response provides a little bit of that painful experience, which hopefully stops the child from a repeat performance. If we neutralize that effect by turning every infraction into a painful experience, we lose a life-saving tool.

The second reason *not* to use shock and awe indiscriminately is because it harms our children. As we already discussed in depth in the previous chapter, volatility is the counterforce to emotional health. If we are always shouting and hitting whenever our children err, they become either timid or aggressive. They need a safe, reasonable, loving environment in which to discover their own strengths and develop the self-discipline to succeed in life. Boundaries, consequences, rewards and praise build children. Yelling and hitting destroy them.

Besides the harm inherent in this method of discipline, there is the fact that it doesn't work for long. If you want to see proof of this fact, walk into a classroom in which a substitute teacher is in charge. If the teacher has entered the classroom ready for a fight, with the idea that, "I'm going to show these kids who's boss right from the start," you can be sure that the classroom will soon be in a shambles. The teacher will be standing in the front of the room screaming helplessly at a bunch of children who are literally laughing at him as they wreak havoc. The more he tries to punish them, the more they push his buttons. They're enjoying the spectacle of an adult out of control.

Don't #2: The Great Debate

We like to believe that our children are logical, intelligent human beings who will respond to the light of our reasoning. Therefore, parents try to win a debate with their children in order to solicit their cooperation. The reason this is a poor strategy is that it signals to the child that he only has to obey if he agrees with our logic:

Mom: Go to sleep. It's your bedtime.

Son: But I'm not tired.

Mom: A boy your age needs nine hours of sleep a night to stay healthy and do well in school.

Son: But I haven't gotten sick the whole year. And I got all A's and B's on my report card.

Mom: Well, let's keep it that way. Now go to bed.

Son: I just want to finish this chapter.

Mom: Finish it tomorrow on the bus. The book is not going anywhere.

Son: It's too noisy on the bus.

Etc., etc. etc. The mother is appealing to her son's logic when the problem really is the child's behavior. He has a bedtime and he is not abiding by it. This discussion may go on for quite awhile, depending on the mother's level of patience and the child's skill at litigation. None of the mother's reasons will change the child's mind because he has his agenda and, like all of us, can only see things from that perspective. The ending will likely sound like this:

Mom (exploding): That's it! End of discussion! Go to bed now! I can't take it anymore! I need you kids to get to sleep and let me get some work done around here in peace! Now move!

Son (in undertone, climbing the stairs): All right! Gosh, I just wanted to finish my chapter…..

As we see in this example, the debate mode causes parents to surrender their authority and rely instead on the child seeing the rightness of their view. Furthermore, it opens the door to an endless debate that will likely end in the parent exploding in frustration. The third and perhaps most damaging aspect of this technique is that it demands that the child see things the parent's way. We can demand that our children *act* in a certain way, but as we discussed in our chapter on Level 5, we foster their emotional health when we accept and validate their feelings and perspective. The son in the above scenario thinks that since he's not tired, he should not have to go to bed. Rather than acknowledging that this is indeed how he sees the situation, the mother tries to convince him that he needs sleep but just doesn't know it. Then he argues that he's engrossed in his reading and wants to see how the chapter ends. Rather than simply sticking to the subject of the bedtime rule and the son's obligation to abide by it, the mother tries to convince him that he's not losing anything by saving the end of the chapter for the next morning.

The debate mode derails our Level 2 and Level 3 goals. Rather than becoming involved in reasons, explanations and logic, we need to simply put into action our behavioral techniques and let the child know that, even if he doesn't concur or see the sense in it, he has to abide by the rules we have set for our household.

This is not to say that there can never be a discussion or that parents should never provide explanations. The point here is that the debate is not a tool for getting a child from Point A to Point B. If you are trying to accomplish something that belongs in a Level 2 or Level 3 category, do not expect debate to accomplish it for you.

Don't #3: Backing Down

If you have told your child that a consequence will follow his misbehavior, you are not "being nice" by letting it go. Instead, you are disabling your entire parenting arsenal. Our goal in Level 2 and 3 is to weave certain rules and behaviors into the fabric of our household: to take them out of the realm of our will against our children's and make them part of nature. "When you do X, Y happens. When you do not do X, the result is Z." If those consequences sometimes do not occur, we defeat our effort. Now our children know that they can "change nature" with enough pleading and kvetching. They see that sometimes, actions don't carry consequences. They also know that we don't always mean what we say.

When this happens, we make our job infinitely harder. The power of our words drains away and our children stop taking us seriously. This means we must work much harder to accomplish our goals. That leads to frustration, anger and everything we are trying to avoid in the atmosphere of our homes.

If you feel that a child needs a little space, give it. But do not give it after the fact, after you've already told him that his continued misbehavior will lead to a certain consequence. For example, a family has a rule that if a child misses his bus, he must go to bed a half-hour earlier the next night. One night, a child has a bad dream and has trouble falling back to sleep. The father can tell him, "You can sleep a little late tomorrow and I'll drive you to school." This does no harm, and in fact helps the child to feel that his father empathizes with him.

But what if, the next morning, the father keeps trying to rouse his son to no avail? He warns, "Remember, if you miss the bus you're going to have to go to bed early tonight," but the child keeps moving at a snail's pace and he misses the bus. Now is *not* the time for the father to say, "Well, it's O.K. because you really didn't sleep well last night." The first case is empathy; the second is inconsistency.

But why does this difference matter? Isn't the second case empathy as well, in which the father realizes, albeit a little later in the game, that his son really wasn't able to rise and shine on that morning? It matters because in the second instance, the father negates the value of his own words. He shows his son that what he says doesn't necessarily come to pass. He erodes his child's trust in him. It is no less damaging for a parent to fail to come through with a consequence than to fail to come through with a reward or a gift.

Because consistency is so very important, the effort we expend "choosing our battles" is vitally important as well. Once we set the ball rolling on a situation that ends in some consequence for the child, we have to be prepared to see it through. We have to realize that he may not cooperate; we may have to get up out of our chair or abandon our post at the kitchen counter or put aside our work or our phone call and play the situation out to the end. We may have to put up with complaints, protests and crying. You may hope that the threat of a consequence will be enough to gain cooperation, but you have to go into the situation knowing that it might not be. If you have no intention of following through, *don't get started!*

For example: A mother is sitting outside watching her 3-year-old, holding her baby in her lap and her cell phone in her hand. The 3-year-old is playing in mud and the mother asks him to stop. "O.K., Aaron, that's one….two…three…did you hear Mommy counting? I said that's one… two…Hello? Leah? Just a minute, I'm dealing with Aaron here….One…two….Aaron, you don't want a time-out, do you?" This mother would be far better off conceding that her son will be getting very dirty and abandoning any semblance of stopping him. The counting, to the son's ears, is just an empty threat. He knows his mother is not getting up off the chair, putting down the baby and the phone and dealing with his mischief. She is trying to manipulate him with remote-control discipline, which is ineffective because it is dishonest.

Consistency requires energy and self-discipline. That's what makes it difficult, and what lures so many parents into the "just this once" mentality. The best rule of thumb is to say "yes" to anything you do not really care enough about to *enforce* a "no." Be sure you really care, because a child has an innate sense of the real limit. If there's wiggle room, he will find it.

Finally, "being nice" does harm to our children's emotional health. They want and need to feel that the grown-ups are in control. If we do not uphold our own rules and maintain a stable, predictable environment for our children, they lack the safe, secure feeling they need to develop healthy personalities. If you listen for it, you can hear a certain pride in a child's voice when he tells a friend, "My mother doesn't let me...." He knows that this means someone cares enough to set limits and keep him safe. The opposite, which you also hear among children is, "My mother *doesn't care* if I...."

Don't #4: Empty Mega-Threats

Hand in hand with the *don't* of inconsistency is the *don't* of threats you will be loath to fulfill. If you make threats that you know you would never fulfill, you do all the damage that inconsistency does. In addition, you add to the child's sense of injustice and insecurity. "Could that really happen? Will my parents really leave me home from the trip to Florida if I get an F on my report card?" What is the child to make of such a threat? Does it mean that the parents think a bad grade is worthy of such a consequence? Does it mean that somewhere deep down inside them, they would like to leave the child home?

Like inconsistency, this type of interaction tends to erode the parent's authority. When you dream up a consequence that the child most likely knows will never happen, you are basically telling him that you have no means by which to get him to do what you want him to do. You are waving a paper dragon in his face, and he knows it's paper.

If you come to the point at which you are using mega-threats, you are probably not following through effectively on your Level 2 and Level 3 strategies. Once you return to those basics and retool your approach, you will most likely find this kind of hyperbolic reaction fading away.

Don't #5: Shaming

Shaming leaves scars. Deep, long-lasting scars. Those scars pose a barrier between a person's heart and all the objects of his heart's affection, including and perhaps pre-eminently, himself. This is what I see time and time again as seemingly successful, functioning adults come to me seeking therapy for the pain and emptiness they feel inside. When a man with a houseful of children and a loving, attentive wife feels empty, it is often because the scar tissue formed in childhood prevents all that love and joy from penetrating.

What exactly is "shaming"? Obviously, it cannot be the same as constructive criticism or discipline. We should not be trapped into thinking that every time we deny our children what they want or insist that they do something they don't want to do, or communicate to them our disapproval of a behavior, that we are scarring them for life. Shaming is an attack on the child's value, his innate worthiness and goodness.

For example, a child leaves his coat on the couch rather than hanging it on the hook as he is supposed to do. The mother might say, "Dovid, the coat belongs on the hook." She might stand there and make sure he hangs it up. She might even call him away from an activity he is enjoying to come and hang up his coat. If he refuses to come, she might use a "One, two, three…" technique to get him moving. None of that is shaming. It all addresses his behavior, not his value as a human being. But what if, instead, the mother sees that coat on the couch for the 10th time this week and says, "Dovid! What's wrong with you? Why can't you follow a simple rule like hanging up your coat?"

In the latter interaction, the mother has raised a terrible, troubling question in her son's heart. *What's wrong with me?* The mother might think it's just a figure of speech and the child understands that she is only expressing her ire, not her belief that her son is innately flawed. And in fact, if such a comment pops out of her mouth rarely, against a backdrop of overwhelmingly positive interactions, it might not pack much of a punch. But if these are the types of reprimands the mother commonly gives, the child's sense of himself is sure to be damaged.

Shaming can also take the form of unfavorable comparisons with other children, either siblings, relatives or friends. "Why can't you keep your room neat like Leah does?" "Why can't you sing at the Shabbos table like Avi does?" "Reuven did great in

Rabbi Schwartz's class. Why can't you?" These types of comments inflict misery. They do not raise a standard toward which the child will strive, but rather, they label him or her as inferior goods.

Once a child begins to believe he is inferior, his standards for himself plummet. He feels that effort is futile, because an inferior person such as himself can never reach the top. Many children who are classified as "at risk" express this vision of themselves. "I'm bad," they say. "That's just the way I am. So what's the point?" They therefore seek acceptance and validation where they can find it.

Even if a child does not reject his parents' way of life, his sense of self becomes destabilized. Without that solid core, the child is open to a long laundry list of mental health and personality issues. He may become introverted, anxious or depressed; in the alternative, he may cover up his weak interior structure with anger, aggression and bravado.

Because so much of our verbal expression has become coarsened in the past few decades, we may not even realize that we are shaming our children. Therefore, I am providing a short, not-at-all complete list of some of the damaging things people say:

What were you thinking?
What do you think you're doing?
Where's your seichel?
Where's your derech eretz?
Where's your yiras Shamayim?
Why are you so lazy?
You're such a space cadet.
Don't be such a slob!

Can't you pay attention?
Why can't you listen?
What's wrong with you?
What were you thinking?

As with all our "don'ts," this one can easily be prevented by effective use of Level 2 and Level 3 techniques. None of the reprimands on the list above address a behavior. Rather, they all accost the child's sense of self. There is nothing the child can do to answer these reprimands, either, because they are not instructions for him to follow; they are attacks on his personality, which he cannot change at will. If we stick to the simple goal of giving our children clear behavioral expectations and enforcing them, shaming never enters the picture.

Don't #6: Teaching Values While Disciplining

There is a saying: "A man convinced against his will is of the same opinion still." This means that you can force someone to agree with you, but in his heart, he will hold fast to his original opinion. I would add that he will probably hold on even harder, because he feels he is under attack. For example, think of a forced apology: "Levi, tell Shimon you're sorry or you're going to your room." Levi might force out a reluctant, "I'm sorry," but in his heart, he will be angrier than ever at Shimon, who has caused his humiliating defeat.

This human dynamic is vital to understand as we work toward our most important goal of raising children imbued with *yiras Shamayim*, and a love of Hashem, His Torah and our fellow Jews. Because people fight back when they are attacked, if any of these values comes across to our children in the form of an attack, their defense may very well be to reject those values. That which we want our children to accept and treasure can only be imparted with sweetness. Their association with these ideals *must* be a positive one.

Several of the examples in the section above about shaming pertain to this point. If a child speaks with *chutzpah,* for instance, there would be some Level 2 consequence for his action. The parent might tell the child, "I don't answer people who don't ask nicely." If this is a habitual occurrence, the parents might have some kind of an incentive chart or reward system for asking nicely. Any of these approaches can be effective to alter the behavior. However, what if the parent instead reacts with a harsh, "Where's your *yiras Shamayim*? How does a Jewish boy talk to his father like that?" Now the child feels that he is defective in the all-important quality of *yiras Shamayim*. *Yiras Shamayim* becomes associated with shame and inadequacy rather than reverence for Hashem. The father has *not* given the child a lesson in *yiras Shamayim*. He has done just the opposite.

A common mistake is associating misbehavior with *kibbud av v'eim*. Of course a child has an obligation to respect his parents and this is an important bedrock of our entire system of belief. Parents are, after all, the conduit through which the next generation receives our spiritual inheritance. Precisely because the chain of *mesorah* depends on *kibbud av v'eim*, we do not want to sour our children's feelings about this mitzvah. We do not want them to associate it with unpleasant consequences. If a child disobeys and deserves a consequence, we have to focus on the behavior and steer clear of associating it with *kibbud av v'eim*.

The time to teach about the mitzvah is when the air is clear, the mood is pleasant and the child is receptive. The way to teach it, as we discussed in Level 4, is through inspirational stories, discussion and example. If a father visits his grandmother in a nursing home, tells fond and admiring stories about his own parents and grandparents and shows them deference and affection, he is teaching *kibbud av v'eim*. If he slaps his *chutzpadik* child and screams, "*Kibbud av!*" he is making the mitzvah abhorrent in the child's eyes.

This point holds for all the values and mitzvos we wish to impart to our children. For instance, if we want to impress on our children the need to acknowledge Hashem's kindness in providing us with food, we cannot do so by punishing them for leaving the table without *bentching*. Then *bentching* becomes a punishment rather than an expression of gratitude. We would get much further in our lesson on gratitude by speaking about the wonder of food and all the work that goes into bringing it to the table. This could be reinforced by a Level 3 incentive program to encourage the children to sit and *bentch* according to their level of ability.

If you want proof of the power of positive associations, consider how many *baalei teshuvah* were inspired to take on a life of Torah observance by the glowing warmth of a Shabbos meal. Says one man: "I watched the father bless his children and I thought to myself, I could spend Friday night driving my kids to the movies, or I could spend it blessing them and eating a meal with them." Says one woman, "I had never seen parents sitting around the table with their grown children singing songs together in the middle of a Saturday afternoon. I was barely able to have a conversation with my parents, and here was this family sitting and singing together."

Of all the Jews in the world, our children need and deserve our *kiruv* most of all.

Don't #7: Explaining Away a Child's Feelings

Never tell a child that he shouldn't feel what he feels. As we discussed in our section on Level 5, your efforts to explain why the situation isn't really so bad, or to direct the child on what the correct response to the situation should be, simply will not work. Just as no one can tell you that a punch in the nose shouldn't hurt because it came from Hashem and will soon be healed, you cannot tell your child that his hurts don't hurt, shouldn't hurt or shouldn't bother him so much. He cannot deny his true feelings, and you are not helping him by insisting that he does so.

First of all, you will lose his trust. He sees that you are not attuned to his inner world, and as he grows older, he will feel less and less willing to spend time convincing you of his reality. Instead, he will keep his feelings to himself or discuss them with someone who seems to understand him.

In addition to the barrier you erect between him and you, you also may erect a barrier within him that prevents him from accepting his own feelings and thoughts. If his feelings are often identified as incorrect or improper, he may begin to doubt himself and his ability to accurately perceive his world. This doubt erodes a person's self-esteem and destabilizes his sense of who he is. In such a state, a person can be easily influenced by others. Instead of knowing what is and is not for him, he can become like malleable Play-doh that is shaped by others' hands.

Even if you do succeed in "explaining away" your child's pain, you deny him the crucial opportunity to process it himself. You will not be there throughout his life to nurse him through every disappointment and worry. You cannot teach a child to swim by carrying him from one end of the pool to the other. He has to expend his own effort and energy, struggling to get to his destination, if he is to build up the skill and strength to handle the challenge. The lack of resilience we so often see among today's children comes at least in part from this parental impulse to smooth out all the rough spots. Empathizing with a child's feelings is not the same as neutralizing them. In fact, if we take a step back and give our children the chance to process their feelings, we often discover that they have much more strength and sense than we realize.

Finally, trying to eliminate your child's painful feelings through logic, *hashkafah* or simple denial of their validity deprives you of one of the most important ways to build a deep bond. You know yourself that those who are there for you in your times of distress are the ones you count as friends. Nothing can bring another person closer to you than being there when needed, *as* needed, sharing your burden rather than challenging your right to feel it. The person who can make you feel understood is priceless, and that is the person we want to be to our children.

The Number One "Do"

Identifying your goals correctly — choosing the right level of interaction — will succeed in most cases in saving you from the "don'ts" described above. Getting your household under control and feeling assured that you have the tools to handle your day-to-day parenting issues is the most important step you can take in eliminating harmful, damaging responses to your children. Love them enough to plan. Love them enough to be consistent. Love them enough to bear the discomfort of their kvetching and righteous indignation when they push against the limits you have set.

It is my deepest hope that through the tools you have found in these pages, you will be able to enhance your joy in parenting and create a home in which warmth, happiness and sanity reign. May we all merit the privilege of raising loving, healthy children who embrace life and its challenges with energy, enthusiasm and trust in Hashem.

Consistency vs. Compassion

You've labored long and hard to get your children's bedtime routine down to a fail-proof, fool-proof procedure. One night, your 8-year-old girl calls for you an hour after lights-out and tells you she can't sleep. You give her some suggestions on ways to fall asleep. A half-hour later, she calls again. Again you insist that the day is done and she should close her eyes and let sleep come. Finally, at 10 p.m., she calls out again. "I can't sleep," she tells you when you arrive at her side, disapproval written all over your face. "Can I come downstairs and have a snack and another story?"

She hasn't tried to prolong her bedtime for months — ever since you instituted your bedtime rules and training program. You wonder, is she worried about something? Excited? You think about how frustrating it is to lie awake in the dark for hours when sleep won't come. You want to give her a break, but you worry:

"Am I being inconsistent? Will this be the beginning of the end of all our hard work?"

In this book, we have placed 110 percent of our emphasis on consistency simply because consistency is so difficult to achieve, and yet is one of the core elements needed for a peaceful and happy home. Parents who succumb to the "just this once" way of thinking often find that they never arrive at their parenting goals.

However, as with many concepts, consistency has its subtleties. We cannot simply be deaf to the pleas of people who need our compassion — especially when those people are our loved ones. Rav Shlomo Wolbe, *zt"l*, who is recognized as one of the leading thinkers in matters of parenting and education, was known to insist that not only is it acceptable for parents to bend, but it is essential, for in doing so, they teach their children that there is compassion in the world. This translates ultimately into faith that Hashem, too, will hear their pleas, even when they may not be deserving. The last thing any parent wants to teach his children is that this is a world without mercy.

When we occasionally, purposefully give in to our children from time to time, we also model that trait for them. They learn that there are times to put aside our own wishes and let another person have his way, just to make that person happy. When they appreciate our act of yielding, they learn what a valuable gift it can be and wish to bestow it on others.

The big question is, how do you do both? How do you maintain the consistency children need in order to live within secure boundaries and understand what is expected of them, and still teach them that sometimes, a sincere plea will be answered even when it breaks a rule?

The answer comes down to one vital point. As long as we use compassion exclusively out of strength and not weakness, we do not have to be concerned that it will lead to a breakdown of discipline. We use compassion out of strength when *we are fully willing and able to say no* and the *only* reason we are saying yes is because we *want* to act compassionately. Let's explore this in more detail.

Who Are You Helping?

If you are facing a situation in which you think that giving in to your child might be the right thing to do, you can check the accuracy of your thought process by asking yourself a few questions:

- "Am I tempted to give in because I can't deal with a conflict right now?" If you're tired or irritable and you just want your child's nagging to stop, you are not acting out of compassion for him. You are feeling compassion for your beleaguered self.
- "Am I afraid of the explosion that will ensue if I deny this request?" Giving in out of fear is not compassion.
- "Do I want to spare my child the effort or frustration of striving to meet this challenge?" If you do something for your child that he can, with reasonable effort, do for himself, you are not helping him. You are depriving him of the experiences that build strength and resilience for his future. Of course, if you see that the child is truly overwhelmed or exhausted, this might be a proper time to give in.

- "Do I feel guilty when I make my child unhappy?" If that is your motivation for yielding, you are once again exercising compassion for yourself rather than your child. If he benefits from the boundaries you've set, you are not being kind by abandoning them.

- "Do I expect something in return for this favor?" If you are giving something in order to get something, you're not really giving. This is not compassion, it's a negotiation strategy. In this realm, you will find that children are not fair-minded negotiating partners. They are unlikely to feel indebted to you for your favor, especially if they are accustomed to getting their way. You know you're on the wrong track if you find yourself saying things like, "How can you act this way when I just let you play for an extra half-hour?"

Giving in order to get something in return builds resentment. Giving to show your child a little extra love and understanding builds a bond of love.

However, making deals is not a bad strategy if it is done with forethought. For instance, you can tell a child explicitly that you are letting him play for an extra half-hour but then he must go to bed right away afterward, and that if he doesn't do his part, he will go to bed a half-hour earlier the next night. This is different than expecting that out of sheer gratitude for your kindness, he will behave with an extra dose of cooperation.

We are only able to make an active decision like this when we have already established firm rules. If a house is chaotic, giving in is not compassion; it's the desperate measure of a parent who cannot get his kids to comply with his rules. Furthermore, it won't teach anything positive to our children. They will not learn kindness from our act of yielding; they will only learn that if they kvetch loud and long enough, they can get what they want. They will not appreciate it as a gift; rather, they will see it as their due.

It is when our home does have firm rules and we are acting out of strength, that we can use the powerful tool of compassion. The word "compassion" means to "feel with" another person. When we feel secure as parents in our ability to run a stable and peaceful household, we can then open up and look at a child with compassion and see that he needs something special at that moment. We feel his worry, his fear, his excitement: whatever it is that is sparking him to seek an exception to the usual rules and routines. Then we can make a proactive decision; we determine that giving in a little in this case will do the child more good than would be done by standing firm.

Don't Say "No" When You Can Say "Yes"

In the same way that fatigue, irritability, impatience or stress are poor reasons to give in, they are also poor reasons to say "no" to something a child wants. When we say "no" for no other reason than that saying "yes" would result in us having to expend more effort than we feel like expending, we place ourselves in a situation in which we are almost guaranteed to give in to nagging. That is because in the simple equation of the situation, upholding our essentially baseless "no" becomes more exhausting than permitting what the child has requested.

For instance, a child asks to be taken outside to play in the backyard. He is too young to play alone. His mother is busy, trying to get some chores done around the house, but the child is bored and demanding attention. The last thing she wants to do is put aside her work and stand outside in the hot sun pushing him on the swing. However, the child won't leave her alone. He nags about going outside. He asks for snacks and toys. He wants to "help" his mother pay bills. She begins to realize that she will have no peace until he gets a chance to run around outside, and so she finally says, "O.K., let's go play outside."

A good rule of thumb is to say yes now to anything to which you would agree to a half-hour from now after a lot of nagging and kvetching. If the child is requesting something that is not bad for him, not against the rules and not too difficult for you to give, do it. Just as parenting requires us to summon the energy to enforce boundaries, it requires us to find the energy to engage, empathize and give to our children. If we do this, we will not find ourselves having to fight meaningless battles just for the sake of consistency.

Bending in the Other Direction

The Rambam teaches that when a person wants to change a character trait, he should bend farther than the "norm" in the opposite direction. This means that if a person tends to be lazy, he should not just put a little more energy into things, but should do everything with full energy and enthusiasm, even if he is faking it at first. If he is stingy, he should not just give a little more, but give all he can and even seek ways to give. The idea is that eventually, when the inspiration begins to wane and the person lapses back in his natural direction, he will hit the moderate "golden mean."

This advice applies to consistency in parenting. In most cases, parents succumb far too easily to the temptation to give in, and they do so for all the wrong reasons that are listed above. Therefore, in this book we have taken the approach that consistency is king. This chapter in no way negates that approach because there is no such thing as compassionate yielding unless there is a backdrop of consistency.

Ultimately, our aim as parents is to do that which benefits, builds and nurtures our children. Every decision we make must be prefaced with the question, "Will this do our child good?" The question is not, "Should I hold firm or give in?" but rather, "What does my child need to grow and be healthy and resilient?" Whether the answer to that is enforcing boundaries or allowing a little variation, compassion for the child should always be the driving force.

Part IV:
The Liebowitz Family

Case Study #1:
A Complete Renovation

When we met Nussi and Ruchi Liebowitz in "Part 1, Your Family," they were dealing with a household that many parents would describe as perfectly normal. Homework and bedtimes were a disaster, the parents got little sleep, the children often erupted into fighting and the Shabbos table was the supreme test of patience. The couple's four children, ranging in age from 7 years to 1 year, were beginning to suffer from the effects of the disorganization and the parents were finding parenthood to be more like an endurance test than a labor of love.

To take hold of the situation, Nussi's and Ruchi's first step was to answer some questions aimed at sorting out and prioritizing the various issues they were facing. As we recorded in Part 1, the challenges they delineated were:

1. The oldest child, Temima, and her 5-year-old brother Daniel were unable to get their homework done. Ruchi was distracted by the demands of the baby, Raizy, and her 3-year-old brother,

Gavriel. Temima drifted off tasks without Ruchi's constant oversight and there was never time left over for Daniel's review of his reading skills.

2. The children never seemed to settle down into bed. They had dozens of requests and constantly found excuses to get up. If the baby woke up, everyone woke up and wanted to get out of bed for various reasons. The parents were up and down all night long.

3. Daniel had a volatile temper and was provoking many fights with Temima, who liked to "mother" him. The Shabbos table was the epicenter of the fighting, which ruined the atmosphere for everyone and deeply disappointed Ruchi and Nussi.

Our goal in counseling was to approach the whole package of challenges. However, we had to begin with one. Which one was a decision for the parents to make.

Step 1: Planning to Plan

Ruchi and Nussi agreed to institute a parenting plan to address the issues of their household. They set aside time on Motzaei Shabbos to focus on what they would do and how they would do it. They agreed that at first, they would meet for a half-hour each week to plan the week ahead and review the week gone by. Once they felt that their new routines were becoming established, they would reduce their meetings to once every two weeks, and then once a month.

They agreed that even if the household turned into Gan Eden, they would maintain at least a once-monthly meeting. In this way, they would be sure to catch new situations that developed as the children's needs changed, and to ensure that they were not reverting to their old, default methods.

In their first meeting, Nussi and Ruchi decided that their first focus would be to improve the homework situation. They felt that if this area became more manageable, it would generate a positive ripple effect on the rest of the children's schedule. Dinner, bedtime and morning routines would all go more smoothly if homework could be completed in a timely fashion. In addition, the problems the children were beginning to encounter in school would be mitigated by arriving prepared.

Step 2: Homework Routine

The first step is to curtail negative behaviors and enforce responsible behaviors in the realm of homework. This creates an immediate shift in the routine, even before long-term training has a chance to take place. Level 2 tools accomplish this paradigm shift. As we recall, this toolbox includes: doing nothing, taking action, using the 1-2-3 technique, establishing "stations," setting rules and pre-setting behaviors.

In Nussi's and Ruchi's first Motzaei Shabbos meeting, they break down the homework situation into its component behaviors and choose tools with which to meet each one. Here is what they planned:

- They established new rules for the house. These were:

  ➤ Homework time begins when Temima comes home (between 4:30 and 5 p.m.). There is no playing until homework is done.

  ➤ Each child has his or her own homework area. Temima works in the dining room and Daniel works at the kitchen table. This eliminates bickering between them. Gavriel goes to the playroom to play or color while the older children are doing homework. This eliminates his distracting provocations of the baby. The baby, Raizy, stays with Ruchi.

  ➢ During homework, Ruchi roves around helping each child as needed.

- The parents decide that they can choose to "do nothing" if a child is spaced out during homework time, as the rule of "no play until homework is done" will serve to motivate them to stay on task.
- Anticipating that Gavriel will inevitably wander out of the playroom and seek attention while homework is going on, they decide to address the behavior by taking action: bringing him by the hand back to the playroom. If that does not work, they will use 1-2-3.
- They decide to pre-set the children's behavior by telling them every morning that homework will be started as soon as Temima gets home and there will be no play until homework is done.

To further reinforce the new homework behaviors and ingrain them in the children, they decide to use a Level 3 tool: They make a "homework chart" for Temima and Daniel that has 10 rows of 10 boxes each. Every night, the children can earn five checks: one for starting right away, one for staying in their homework area for the first 10 minutes, one for the next 10 minutes, one for the last 10 minutes and one for completing the homework. Gavriel gets a chart for staying in the playroom. When the charts are done, the parents will take the children out for ice cream.

- Sunday morning, they print the charts and explain the new rules to the children.
- Monday morning, they start the day by pre-setting Temima, telling her what will happen when she comes home from school.
- At 4 p.m. and 4:15 p.m., Ruchi pre-sets Gavriel and Daniel by telling them what is going to happen at 4:30.
- At 4:30, Temima comes home and all the children scamper off to their stations. Ruchi uses praise to reinforce their behavior. She makes a big announcement, using the **TEFS** (See Chapter 3) formula: "All of you ran to stations exactly on time! I'm so proud of you! I feel so calm and happy when you all do that!" She takes her marker and enthusiastically makes a check for each child.
- A few minutes after homework begins, Temima asks for help. At 4:40, Ruchi makes the second big announcement and proudly confers checks for 10 minutes of sticking with homework.
- Things are going well. At 4:50, there is another round of checks.
- At 5, they get the last check for the 10-minute time period as well as a check for the completed homework. When Nussi gets home, Ruchi makes a big deal of telling him how well the children did. He admires their respective charts.

As the week goes on, Ruchi runs into some trouble spots. Gavriel comes out of his area, Temima doesn't always start on time without some prodding, and sometimes the homework isn't finished in a timely way.

At the next meeting, the parents discuss what has worked and what needs fine-tuning. They notice that they were not reacting consistently when Gavriel came out of his station. They decide to put more focus on that behavior. They also decide to do more pre-setting with Temima on the goal of starting on time. They also decide to focus on validating Temima when she complains that homework is too hard and that it's not fair that she can't play right away.

During the course of the next week, Nussi and Ruchi carry out the plan with the modifications they have introduced, and it works quite well. Using a calm and consistently enforced time-out, Ruchi is able to get Gavriel to stay in the playroom while the older children do their homework. The pre-setting helps Temima adopt a habit of starting homework right away. Homework is becoming something of a routine event in the household; it no longer feels like a massive, daily struggle! Meanwhile, the kids are excitedly watching their charts fill and talking about what ice-cream flavor they will order.

Step 3: Bedtime

With the homework situation greatly improved, Nussi and Ruchi set their sights on the next frontier: bedtime. Once again, the parents turn to their Level 2 tools to make immediate changes in the children's behavior.

- They establish a set of bedtime rules:

  - ➢ Gavriel and Daniel go to bed at 7. Temima's bedtime is 7:30.
  - ➢ All three children must be upstairs and getting ready for bed at 6:45. Bedtime stories are at 7 p.m. for all the children.
  - ➢ Every child will have two chances to come out of bed and ask for something (a drink, the bathroom, etc.). The parents intend to phase this out when the children become accustomed to staying in bed. If a child comes out of bed a third time, his/her door gets closed and the lights go out.

> ➢ Children who aren't upstairs getting ready for bed on time lose their bedtime story. Children who aren't in bed on time lose one of the "chances" to get out of bed. If a child is more than 15 minutes late, he/she loses the second "chance." If a child is more than 30 minutes late, he/she goes to bed with the door closed and the lights out.

- The parents decide that if a child comes out of his/her bed but stays upstairs, they will do nothing. It's not worth the energy to insist on perfection.
- The parents will pre-set the behaviors to help get the children acclimated to them.
- As they did with their homework plan, Nussi and Ruchi also institute Level 3 training to reinforce the new behaviors.
- They start with a chart. Each child can earn 3 checks per night: One for being upstairs on time, one for being in bed on time and one for staying in bed (not coming out more than the times allowed).
- When the charts are completed (50 checks per child), the parents will purchase a new bedtime book for each child. If the parents feel that the behaviors are not yet solid at the end of the chart, they can continue their training with a second chart.
- All the children can earn a bonus check on any night that, if the baby starts crying, they remain lying down in bed. The parents do a practice session where they role-play. Ruchi climbs into Gavriel's bed and Nussi, pretending to be the baby, starts crying loudly. Ruchi stays in bed and gets TEFS praise and a check. Gavriel, Temima and Daniel each get to practice this routine twice, each time earning a check on their real charts.

Sunday night, things go well. The kids are upstairs on time, in bed on time and they are lapping up the checks and the TEFS praise. They all use both chances to come out of bed.

At 8:15, the baby wakes up and Ruchi rushes upstairs to Gavriel's room. She sees him stirring in bed, and before he has a chance to get up, she gives him abundant TEFS praise for staying in bed. She stands in Gavriel's room holding a marker for the next 5 minutes as the baby falls back asleep, and when the episode is over, she gives him the extra check. Gavriel is delighted.

The next day, Gavriel's extra check is a huge topic of conversation. Nussi theatrically complains that it's not fair, that he also wants an extra check. Gavriel gets a mitzvah note describing his great feat. The parents also use this opportunity to pre-set Gavriel's behavior for the coming night.

The next night things go well again. The baby doesn't awaken. However, on the following night, Daniel is late going upstairs to get ready for bed. Therefore, he loses his bedtime story. He complains loudly about this consequence, and Ruchi validates him, reflecting the disappointment he feels. Daniel then bargains to swap a "coming out chance" for the story. Ruchi accepts the deal.

One night, Gavriel comes out and doesn't go back to bed when told. Nussi gives him a "1-2-3" chance to comply with the rule, but he balks. As a consequence, he goes to bed with his door closed and the lights off. Despite a lot of crying and pleading, the parents hold their ground, knowing that it will pay off.

The next night, Gavriel comes out again. This time, when Nussi counts a 1-2-3 chance for him to comply with the rule, Gavriel rushes back to bed. Both parents are astonished at how simply the problem is resolved.

At the next meeting, the parents decide to offer the children the option of trading a "coming out chance" for a check. They also note that the homework routine is on track, and that they have been effectively applying the 1-2-3 technique with Gavriel and Daniel for other behaviors.

Looking into the future, Ruchi and Nussi plan to eventually establish a Level 3 program to curtail fighting, to help Daniel's control his temper and to improve the Shabbos table atmosphere. However, for the present, they want to concentrate on solidifying their gains in the homework and bedtime routines.

So Far, So Good

Looking back over the four weeks since they have started their Five-Level Parenting plan, Nussi and Ruchi see real progress. There is a greater sense of order in the house. Managing the family seems easier and the tension has evaporated. Most importantly, the parents feel that they have a plan: steps to take when challenges arise. This alone makes them feel comfortable and confident. They are also finding that the parenting tools are becoming second nature. They are lavishing much more TEFS praise on their children, "catching them being good." In addition, they are ready with the tools of 1-2-3, doing nothing or taking action as the situation demands.

Four Months Later

Nussi and Ruchi haven't had a Motzaei Shabbos meeting for a little more than a month. They realize that they are seeing a decline in the children's behavior. Bedtime and homework are beginning to slide back to the old days. The parents hold a meeting and assess the situation.

When they begin to analyze what has been going on, they realize that they have been expecting the children to maintain their routines on their own. When that doesn't happen, the parents have been reverting to the old "techniques" of yelling, empty threats, bargaining and cajoling. They decide to restore the boundaries they had set, and to maintain them firmly and calmly.

The next two days are difficult as the children run over the boundaries and encounter the consequences. They find themselves losing playtime when homework isn't done on time, and going to bed with doors closed and lights turned out when they balk at their bedtime routine. They are outraged to find that the parents are back in control and they do plenty of crying and complaining at the unfairness of it all. Ruchi and Nussi validate their sense of injustice, but they don't back down. Within two days, the children are back on track.

This pattern continues. When the parents put their energy into managing the household, the household becomes manageable. When they slack off, the routines begin to slip. They eventually notice the backsliding; then they regroup and get back on track. Gradually, the Five-Level system and its tools become second nature to the parents and the children as well. These tools will serve them well as their children grow older, the family grows and the children's needs change.

We see that the job is never finished. The household is always in need of vigilance and maintenance. The difference is that now,

Ruchi and Nussi are proactively running a household rather than dashing about madly trying to calm the chaos and control the damage. Moreover, the children are thriving. They have the security of knowing what is expected of them and feeling that their parents care enough to energetically engage in raising them.

Case Study #2:
"Operation Temima"

Now that the Liebowitz household is operating smoothly and the Five-Level Parenting tools are becoming second nature, Nussi and Ruchi turn their focus toward more specific issues:

- A great deal of friction in the household comes from Temima's bossiness toward her brother.
- Not only does this trait provoke her brother, the frequent recipient of her "motherly concern," but it also interferes with her social success at school.
- Perhaps because of this, she has become very emotional and easily overwhelmed by any negative interaction with friends.
- In addition, she still lags in getting started with homework and other tasks. She is developing into a talented procrastinator.

The parents decide to start with the situation that has the most direct impact on their household, and that is Temima's insistence on "mothering" Daniel. They approach the problem through Level 3, with the goal of helping her form new habits in her response to her brother's behavior. They want her to learn *not* to see his behavior, or more specifically, his misbehavior, as her problem to address. However, children have a much easier time learning and practicing what they *should* do instead of what they must refrain from doing. As we learned in Level 3, the best strategy is to "flip the behavior," which means identifying the positive behavior that is the opposite of the unwanted habit. We then break the desired habit into doable steps that the child is capable of performing.

Ruchi and Nussi put some real thought into figuring out what the "flip side" of bossiness would be. They come up with the goal of "letting him be." The next step is to break down that relatively amorphous goal into smaller, concrete steps that Temima could understand and achieve. The steps they establish are:

1. Notice when you have the feeling that you want to boss Daniel.

2. Stop and take a deep breath.

3. Say to yourself, *It's not my job to tell him what to do. I'm letting it be.*

To reinforce the new habit, the parents set aside a jar in which they will put one quarter every time Temima reports that she follows the three-step process. When the jar is filled, Temima will go shopping with her mother for a gift of her choosing with the money she has earned.

As we discussed in the chapter on Level 3, children commonly go out of their way to create situations in which they can earn the promised reward. For instance, Temima might see Daniel spill some of his drink at dinner and report to her mother, "I saw Daniel spill his drink and I felt like telling him to wipe it up but instead I let it be!" It's possible that she had no interest at all in Daniel's spill, but found in the episode an opportunity to "game the system" and get an extra quarter deposited in her jar. This is not a negative, because our goal is to encourage the child to rehearse the behavior as often as possible until it becomes second nature. As long as she is exercising her "letting it be" muscle, everyone wins.

The morning after Nussi and Ruchi decide on this course of action, they go to the bank and obtain rolls of quarters. They have learned that training programs only work when the promised rewards are given on the spot and consistently. When they get home, they explain the plan to Temima. They allow her to practice the three-step "letting it be" process three times, with Nussi playing the role of Daniel. She gets to hear the satisfying clink of a quarter in her jar each time she practices her response, and is now looking forward to trying the procedure out for real.

On the Level 2 enforcement side of the equation, the parents establish a "bossiness station" to which Temima will be directed if they observe her being bossy. They explain that this is not a punishment; it is a way to help her when she is having trouble stopping herself. The station is her room, where she is free to play with toys, color and entertain herself; it's meant to be a change of venue, not deprivation. Nevertheless, if she doesn't go to her station when her parents direct her to do so, they will use the 1-2-3 time-out method as a consequence.

With all the pieces of the program in place, the parents step back and let life happen. That evening, when Ruchi tells Daniel to pick up a toy he has left on the floor, he ignores her request. Ruchi observers Temima talking to herself. Then Temima turns to her mother and says, "I just now felt like saying, 'Daniel, you have to go pick up your toy right now!' But I stopped myself and I said 'I'm letting it be!'" Ruchi heaps praise on Temima, using the TEFS formula for effective praise (see Level 3) that truly builds a child's sense of self-worth. She also puts a quarter in the jar.

At bedtime, Daniel is slow about going upstairs to get into his pajamas. Ruchi sees by Temima's facial expression that she is about to issue a motherly rebuke, but the expression suddenly changes and Temima's mouth softly works through her new self-message. Again she reports to Ruchi that she has overcome her urge and succeeded in letting go. The praise and the quarters are beginning to pile up.

Of course, the problem is not yet licked. At breakfast, Daniel pours himself an overflowing bowl of cereal and Temima tells him, "That's too much, Daniel. Now there won't be enough for everyone else!" Ruchi jumps right in. She doesn't hesitate or worry about the reaction she might have to endure when she uses her Level 2 tool because she has already seen how quickly and effectively these tools work. "Please go to your bossiness station now, Temima," she says.

"But I wasn't bossing, Mommy!" Temima objects. "I was just *telling* him that it's not fair..."

"That's one....two...." Ruchi begins. Temima is already on her way to her room.

As the days progress, Temima begins to naturally follow the only logical course left open to her. She wants to earn her rewards.

She wants to avoid wasting time in her bossiness station. She wants and loves the abundant praise she gets for exercising self-control, and even though she may not yet realize it, she benefits from the greatly reduced friction between her and Daniel. They even begin to seek each other out as playmates, much to their parents' amazement.

That week after Shabbos, Nussi and Ruchi sit down to review the week's progress. They can hardly believe that the constant fighting between Temima and Daniel, which had been ongoing for several years, has nearly disappeared in a week. On the other hand, they *can* believe it, because they have seen so many other seemingly intractable problems dissolved by the simple method of proactive parenting. They agree to continue focusing on this issue for the time being.

As the next week unfolds, Temima's jar is filling up. Ruchi notices that her daughter has become so acclimated to "letting it be" that it is becoming her natural response. Temima often does not even notice Daniel's doings anymore. However, Ruchi notices Temima's new attitude and recognizes it with enthusiastic TEFS praise and quarters. This is essential in order for Temima to gain traction with her improved behavior. If she stops getting praise and attention as a result of her success, she will have no incentive to maintain it. The fact that it is becoming easier for her is *more* of a reason for Ruchi to keep praising and rewarding.

After five weeks, Ruchi cannot fit another quarter into Temima's jar. Bursting with pride, mother and daughter take their 78 quarters to the bank to exchange for dollars. Temima requests a trip to the arts and crafts store, where she buys herself a box of colored paper and markers. The next day, Ruchi writes a mitzvah note to Temima's *morah* detailing her daughter's great achievement. That evening after dinner, the mother calls both grandmothers to spread the news and allow Temima to receive their congratulations.

After homework time, Temima takes out her new paper and markers and makes a storybook. The theme is "letting it be." She asks Ruchi to read the story to the family as that night's bedtime story. By this time, there is absolutely nothing about bossing Daniel that can compete with the rewards of "letting it be."

The next time Nussi and Ruchi meet to discuss their parenting program, they agree that Temima has truly overcome her bossiness with her brother. However, the new habits have not yet translated into more appropriate interactions with her classmates. They decide to make that the next goal.

Cashing in on Temima's newfound abilities, Ruchi explains to her that she can have a happier time with friends, just as she now has a happier time with her brother. All she has to do is practice her "letting it be" skill with her friends in school. Temima understands readily what's expected of her. The steps no longer need to be broken down.

Ruchi makes a chart and tells Temima that she can get a check any day she comes home from school and reports a situation in which she "let it be." When she has earned one complete week of consecutive checks, she can invite her three best friends on a Sunday for a celebration. By the end of the second week, Temima has earned her reward. When her friends come over for the promised celebration, which includes ice-cream sundaes and a trip to the petting zoo, Ruchi can see immediately that Temima's social skills have improved.

The next goal for "Operation Temima" is to help her fight her tendency to procrastinate. The parents realize that more *zerizus* (alacrity and enthusiasm) will help all their children, and so they make this a family project. *Zerizus* becomes a hot topic in the Liebowitz home.

The parents start with a Level 4 approach to this issue, using inspiration and role-modeling to encourage their children to value these important traits. At the Shabbos table, they discuss the importance of acting on tasks right away. They tell a tale of someone who experienced a miracle as a result of forcing himself out of bed and off to shul on a cold winter morning. They also talk about the loss involved in missing out on a mitzvah. When Nussi steps out the door to Minchah on Shabbos, Ruchi exclaims enthusiastically to all the children "Wow, look at how much *zerizus* Tatty had when it came time for Minchah! He left right away!"

On Level 3, they praise any child who responds right away to a request or performs a task without being asked. They focus as much praise as possible on Temima, even when she is performing tasks she usually does without prompting. For instance, she always hangs up her coat when she comes home from school. Nevertheless, as part of the parents' training program, Ruchi notices and praises her: "Wow, Temima, it's so responsible of you to hang up your coat as soon as you take it off! That really helps keep the house neat. I love how you didn't even wait a second but instead did it right away with *zerizus*!"

They also start a *zerizus* chart on which the children are able to win checks when they report that they wanted to say, "I'll do it later," but instead, they do the task right away. The payoff for a full line of checks is a special outing alone with Nussi on Motzaei Shabbos. Soon, the children are rushing around the house doing all their chores and tasks at comical speed.

Finally, on the Level 2 front, the parents make sure to enforce Temima's prompt attention to tasks. Since getting started on homework is an especially important piece to the puzzle, Ruchi directs her to her homework spot, sometimes even taking her by the hand, as soon as she gets home. If she procrastinates, Ruchi uses "one-two-three, time-out" to force the issue.

The final frontier for "Operation Temima" is to work on her high level of drama and distress whenever she feels slighted by friends. Nussi and Ruchi see this clearly as a Level 5 issue, requiring abundant empathy and validation of her emotional reaction. They now understand that their default responses of, "I'm sure she didn't mean to hurt your feelings," or "It's not such a tragedy!" are counterproductive. However, they also worry that allowing her to emote at full throttle will only encourage further drama. Nevertheless, they are willing to try an empathetic approach and see what evolves from there.

The first opportunity to try the new approach is not long in coming. On Friday, Temima comes home from school slouched and morose. "Temima, you look like something is bothering you," Ruchi says to her. "Is it something I can help you with?"

Temima begins to cry. "No one can help me," she states dramatically. "Because no one can make Mindy invite me for

Shabbos afternoon! I heard her invite Atara and Layala, but she didn't invite me. Then I said, 'Mindy, can I come too?' and she said her mother only lets her have two guests on Shabbos. And she's supposed to be my friend! I don't have any friends!" Temima collapses into sobs.

Ruchi fights off her strong impulse to explain away Temima's pain. She is committed to the empathetic, validating approach. She holds Temima while the child sobs, and murmurs to her daughter, "Oh, this must have been so sad for you. Look how hard you're crying. I really wish you had been invited."

"They all hate me!" Temima pronounces. "Daniel's my only real friend!"

"You feel so left out," Ruchi echoes. "That's such a sad feeling. I wish everyone in the school would want to be your friend!"

And so it goes. Little by little, Temima's hysteria settles into sniffles. Ruchi says, "I wish we could have the biggest Shabbos party in the world and everyone you know could come and no one would feel left out! We could have a hundred girls. No....a thousand!"

Temima laughs. "We can't fit a thousand girls in our house," she says. "They'll have to play in our yard. And the Cohen's yard too. And the Birnbaum's yard, too!"

Ruchi gives Temima a hug and a kiss and tells her that she hopes she will have a nice Shabbos anyway. She suggests that perhaps she could invite a different friend over and Temima agrees.

Discussing the interchange later with Nussi, Ruchi realizes that Temima recovered from her distress far faster than she had in previous instances. In addition, on other occasions when Ruchi had suggested that her daughter invite over a friend other than the one who had hurt her, Temima rejected the idea. This time, Temima has time to process her sadness and the idea of a different friend does not seem like a quick fix to make the problem go away, but rather, an alternative she is ready to consider.

The Liebowitz parents are sold on the power of empathy after this incident. They continue to use it, not only with Temima but with the other children as well. After several weeks, they realize that Temima's dramatic outbursts have diminished noticeably. She is learning to process her emotions on her own.

At this point, Nussi and Ruchi's major goals with Temima have been achieved. Meanwhile, they continue to integrate all five levels of parenting tools into their household. The children know what to expect, and the parents know that they can indeed have expectations of their children. They sometimes think back on what they considered "normal," which strengthens their motivation to stay on course. The family is growing together.

Case Study #3:
Dealing With Daniel

Now that Temima has gotten control of her urge to boss her younger brother, Daniel, a major source of provocation is nearly gone from the Liebowitz home. However, Daniel's explosive, inflexible nature has not disappeared. He still suffers from a very low threshold for frustration which, when crossed, sends him careening out of control. The trigger can be anything: his reading homework is too hard; he doesn't like what's for dinner; the baby is making noise while he's trying to read; it's time to put his toys away and get ready for bed. His quick temper turns any of these small irritations into a blowup.

However, Nussi and Ruchi have already seen that seemingly inborn personality traits can be altered. They never imagined that Temima could let go of her bossiness, but she did. Can Daniel learn to defuse before he blows up? They decide to try the same method they used successfully with Temima, "flipping the behavior" and breaking it down into doable steps.

First, they more precisely define what they are hoping to accomplish. They come up with three "subgoals" of the overall effort to improve Daniel's self-control. These are:

- Reacting calmly when he feels angry or frustrated;
- Being patient when things take longer than he expects;
- Becoming more flexible when situations change and do not go as he anticipates.

The first goal, reacting calmly in the face of anger or frustrations, seems to the parents to be the best place to start, as it may help to achieve the other two goals as well. Rather than trying to teach Daniel to simply hold himself back, bite his tongue and sit on his hands, they flip the behavior so that he has proactive steps to take when he is feeling provoked. Instead of "don't lose your temper," Daniel will learn to "keep calm." He will do so by following three steps:

- Say to yourself, *I'm feeling pretty angry/frustrated*.
- Decide if you want to ignore the thing that's bothering you, walk away from it or tell an adult.
- Do the action you've chosen.

The parents also recognize that Level 3 pre-setting can be helpful. For instance, one frequent trigger for Daniel's outbursts is his younger brother Gavriel's interference with his games. Therefore, the parents rehearse this situation with Daniel and "program" him ahead of time to take the appropriate actions when it happens. Another trigger is Ruchi's dinner menu. Daniel hates being "trapped in *fleishigs*" and therefore tends to explode when a meat meal is served. Therefore, Ruchi decides to pre-set him for this situation as well, going as far as offering him a snack of cereal and milk when he comes home from school so that he won't miss his favorite bedtime snack.

Realizing that Daniel's frustrations are real to him and the anger he feels is overpowering, the parents agree to offer him more Level 5 empathy and validation of his emotions. In addition, they decide to employ Level 4 "teaching and inspiration" to convey the value of controlling anger and maintaining calm. Nussi searches for and finds some stories to tell at bedtime which describe how people, both the great and the ordinary, maintained their calm against difficult odds. He specifically wants Daniel to comprehend the impact of angry words on their recipient, and the kindness entailed in considering others' feelings.

With all of these plans laid out, the parents get ready to institute their Level 3 program. They create a chart on which Daniel can earn checks by employing the three-step process they have devised for him. They show Daniel the chart and explain to him that its purpose is to help him stay calm. Then they explain the three-step process. He can earn a check every time he reports to his parents that he used the three steps and stayed calm. When he earns 50 checks, he will receive a new Lego set.

Nussi and Ruchi rehearse the three-step process with Daniel twice. He proudly performs his part and receives two checks on his chart. The next morning, he can hardly wait to get to school and try out his new skills. When he gets home, he relates two stories of heroic self-control to Ruchi. She responds with abundant TEFS praise and two grandly inscribed checks on his chart.

That evening, Nussi notices Gavriel approaching the area where Daniel has set up his Legos. "O.K., Daniel, here comes Gavriel. Time to *not* be calm," Nussi teases. "Not me," Daniel says. "I'm going to tell an adult. Tattie, can you get Gavriel away from my Legos?" Nussi complies and then makes a big announcement that Daniel has earned another check for being calm. "Now, his new name is Mr. Calm," Nussi says.

Daniel is thrilled with his triumph and his new identity. He uses his new skills wherever and whenever there's an opportunity. In three days, he has earned 15 checks and his reactions to the frustrations of life have become far-more moderate.

However, Ruchi notes that he sometimes seems to be struggling against real negative emotions. When she sees that happening, she makes sure to give him some private time to vent his emotions. She validates his feelings, sometimes coaxing him to reach deeper into the source of his displeasure or frustration. Once he has cried, complained and mourned over his disappointed expectation and experienced his parents' empathy for his pain, he is ready to move past it.

As the weeks go by, Ruchi notices that Daniel processes his anger much faster and feels it less intensely. He is becoming accustomed to weathering a certain amount of adversity, realizing on his own that it isn't the end of the world.

Nussi realizes that the universe has truly shifted one day when he can't find his car keys. He is late for shul and is becoming frustrated, riffling through drawers, piles of odds and ends and coat pockets with increasing agitation. Daniel, observing his father's fraying patience, says, "Tattie, you can do the three steps!" Nussi realizes that this is his moment. "You know, you're right," he says. "I choose to ignore my lost keys and get a ride with Mr. Pearl."

"Now you can be Mr. Calm Number 2!" Daniel tells him. Daniel takes only two weeks to fill his chart, and the impact is clear for the family to see. Now he wants a new challenge so that he can earn more checks and another Lego set.

At this point, the parents decide to turn their attention to the specific skill of patience. Again they break down the desired behavior into three microskills.

- Say to yourself, *I'm having trouble waiting (for something to be finished or to start)*.
- Ask an adult to show you five more minutes on your watch.
- Say to yourself, *I can wait for five minutes calmly*.

Nussi's and Ruchi's first step is to buy Daniel a digital watch. They show him how to read the minutes, and then they do various activities for five minutes to help him understand how long that is. Next, they make him a chart. Whenever he feels that something is taking too long to begin or too long to be finished, he can use his five-minute procedure to stay calm. He receives a check for every five-minute period during which he waits calmly. If something takes more than five minutes, he gets a check for each five-minute period he waited calmly. With 50 checks, Daniel gets a breakfast at the bagel shop with Nussi.

Daniel is thrilled with his new watch and his new chart. He is suddenly offering to be the last in line for the swings at the playground, earning himself two checks for a 10-minute wait.

By giving Temima the window seat on a 20-minute drive to the supermarket, he earns four points; he willingly waits for the ride home to claim that coveted spot. Daniel's paradigm shift is immediate. "Now I'm also Mr. Patient," he tells Ruchi.

Taking nothing for granted, Ruchi and Nussi make sure to give Daniel plenty of praise whenever they notice him exercising patience in any circumstances. They also continue using Level 4 stories and role-modeling to help Daniel see this trait as a hallmark not only of a well-behaved child, but of a great person.

Once Daniel is conversant in the skills his parents want to impart to him, they are comfortable dealing with his slipups in a simple, Level 2 manner. He now knows what is expected of him and he can perform. Therefore, a simple, "Daniel, calm, please. One…two…three," is enough to set him back on track.

The Liebowitz family has come a long way from where they were when they first came to my office exhausted, confused and disappointed by the atmosphere of their home. Ruchi relates that she realizes how much things have changed when she sits outdoors with the other mothers, watching their children play. "They yell a dozen times, 'Get out of the street!' and the kids run right back. They tell them that it's time to go inside a half-hour before they really need to, and an hour later, they're still trying. That was me. I don't want to berate anyone else, but I know now that it doesn't have to be this way. It took a lot of effort. It still does. But I can now say I enjoy my kids."

In Conclusion

L ike the Liebowitz family, you, too, can use the tools in this book to create a "business plan" for the greatest enterprise of your life: raising your children. There's no magic involved, no extraordinary skills or personality traits, no financial investment beyond the simple rewards and incentives you might offer. In theory, it's a very simple, straight road from exhaustion and chaos to sanity and satisfaction.

In practice, it's also a straight road. But there's a challenge: to consistently rally the energy and focus we need to stay on the right path. It's not uncommon when using Five-Step Parenting for an inner voice to show up that says, *I don't have the patience/energy/ time to do this right now*. However, if you can notice that voice for what it is, just a voice, and stick to the plan, you will find that in just a few days or weeks, your child-management efforts will pose far less of a drain on your patience/energy/time. Far more often, you'll find yourself in the rewarding role of nurturing children rather than the frustrating role of crisis management.

This transformation is doable! You only need to stick to the process, stay focused on the results and most of all, keep in mind the long-term benefit your proactive parenting will bestow on your children. It's a matter of seeing parenting as a process rather than a natural state of being. With that perspective, you and your spouse together can build a family that meets its highest potential. Within it, your children will reach their highest potential as kind-hearted, responsible human beings and faithful members of Klal Yisrael.

As the Liebowitz family discovered, so much more is in the parents' control than they may believe. Nevertheless, as every Jewish parent knows, the real control is in Hashem's hands. We do our best and He does the rest. Therefore, the most important ingredient in our success is our heartfelt prayers. Pray for the strength and wisdom to be a good parent to your children. Pray for your husband or wife. Pray for the health – mental, spiritual and physical – of your children. Ask Hashem to guide them along the right path in life, to open the right doors for them and connect them with good people. Ask that they bring you and Him abundant *nachas*.

And may your prayers be answered!